THE GOLD GUIDES

CHÂTEAUX OF THE LOIRE

SUMMARY

Project and editorial conception: Casa Editrice Bonechi
Publication manager: Serena de Leonardis
Picture research, graphics and cover: Serena de Leonardis
Video layout: Vanni Berti, Bernardo Dionisio
Editing: Patrizia Fabbri and Simonetta Giorgi
Maps: Studio Grafico Daniela Mariani - Pistoia
The coat of arms of the Loire was prepared by Roberto Ciabani
Texts: Simone d'Huart, Chief Conservator, Archives of France; Martine Tissier de Mallerais,
Conservator of the Château and Museums of Blois; Jean Saint-Bris, Conservator of the
Château of Clos-Lucé; Henri de Linarés, Conservator of the International Museum of the
Hunt-Gien; Daniel Oster, Institut de France; Monique Jacob, Conservator of the Museums,
Château of Saumur; François Bonneau, Conservator of the Château of Valençay;
François Lemaire, Delegate General of the Association "Les Châteaux Rénaissants"
Publisher's Texts: Patrizia Fabbri, Maurizio Martinelli, Giuliano Valdes

Photography
Gianni Dagli Orti, Andrea Fantauzzo, Paolo Giambone and Andrea Pistolesi
Photos on pages 36 below, 37 above right: Arnoux-Serreau
Photo on page 136: J.P. Klein (courtesy of the Château of Montsoreau)

© Copyright by Casa Editrice Bonechi, via Cairoli, 18/b, 50131 Florence, Italy
E-mail: bonechi@bonechi.it

Distributed by: OVET-Paris
13, rue des Nanettes - 75011 Paris - Phone 43 38 56 80

Printed in Italy by Centro Stampa Editoriale Bonechi.

ISBN 88-476-0841-4

www.bonechi.com

INTRODUCTION

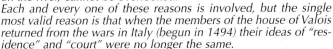

*I*t seems natural to wonder why so many châteaux are situated along a river and its tributaries on a patch of land 200 kilometers long and 100 wide.

The reason may lie partly in the clear blue skies and peaceful valley of a river that runs through the heart of France, far from troubled frontiers.

On the other hand, the fact that the Hundred Years' War (1337-1453), in which the idea of a nation came to the fore, was resolved here, on the river, cannot be overlooked.

Each and every one of these reasons is involved, but the single most valid reason is that when the members of the house of Valois returned from the wars in Italy (begun in 1494) their ideas of "residence" and "court" were no longer the same.

Their castles, which up to then had been little more than rude strongholds, had lost their raison d'être, for peace at home was now ensured and the invention of artillery had turned walls that seemed impregnable into fragile screens.

Charles VIII, Louis XII and Francis I had assimilated the Italian model in which the measure of royal power was no longer armed might but culture, elegance, ostentation, a daily life immersed in luxury and a love of the spectacular and of being seen.

Louis XII had called Laurana and Niccolò Spinelli from Italy and had left the palace of the Louvre for Plessis-lès-Tours. This is how it all began. Italian culture had made a breach.

When Charles VIII returned from Naples in 1495, Italian artists followed in his wake. The old strongholds began to be opened up, the walls were emptied and light was finally allowed to enter.

Only a few characteristic elements of the castle-fortress still remained: the machicolations, for example, were transformed into ornamental motifs (Amboise, Chaumont, Chenonceau, Azay-le-Rideau, Chambord). Openings were surrounded by friezes, and chimneys made their appearance on the roofs as real sculptural elements.

Landscape gardening, with its fountains, ornamental waterworks, hedges alternated with flowerbeds, was created as an art together with the art of living. Among the artists who accompanied Charles VIII when he returned from Italy was Fra' Pacello da Marcogliano, the inventor of open spaces, who had been carried away from the court of Naples and who had never forgotten the precise green geometrical patterns of the Sicilian orange groves.

When he was in Naples, Charles VIII had lived in Poggioreale which was more like a stage set for fêtes and periods of relaxation than a castle. When he returned to France, he transformed the old fortress of Amboise into a series of halls, gardens, terraces, galleries.

Charles d'Amboise, sent to Milan by order of his king, Louis XII, returned overcome by the splendid life at court and the pomp and ceremony of the Visconti court and he, too, transformed his castle of Meillant.

This was when the Loire acquired a central role in the arts. The

flamboyant style of the châteaux is a new dimension in the art of the court.

The nobility and the new wealth of the bourgeoisie gravitated around the court. Bankers and financiers such as Berthelot at Azay-le-Rideau, Bohier at Chenonceau, were so powerful that the kings graciously accepted loans from them.

And there were also merchants like Jacques Coeur, whose ships and whose storehouses overflowing with silks, cotton, spices and products of the Orient can still today be admired in the stained glass windows in Bourges.

And there was also Salviati, the Italian banker, whose chief merit in addition to making loans to nobles and kings is that of having had a daughter, Cassandra, who served as inspiration for Ronsard, the greatest Renaissance poet in French literature. Peace at home and the absence of tensions along the borders permitted the kings to carry on a policy of prestige and splendor which was externalized in the lacy pile of stone which is Chambord, and which, like Versailles later on, was meant to dazzle Europe. Even the ambassador of the Serenissima was left breathless – and he came from Venice. And the nobles sought to emulate the life style of the king.

Charles V.

The Amboise family built Chaumont; the house of Hurault, Cheverny. The cities began to be built in the style which still survives in their historical centers: Tours, Blois, Angers, Orléans, cities that seem to have been carved, not constructed.

It was pure chance that on May 29, 1418, the history of the Loire as a royal residence began with the flight of the dauphin of France (the future Charles VII), who sought refuge in Bourges from the Burgundian hordes. Had they wanted to, the kings who succeeded him could have returned to live in Paris once it had been reconquered. Instead they chose to live on the banks of the river. And thus for 170 years, one of the most resplendent periods in the history of France unravelled along the valley of the Loire.

Charles VII.

The river was a vital waterway along which the square sails of the boats and barges slowly moved.

It was the natural way to the sea which it meets at Nantes. Silks, spices, pearls, precious stones, works of art, war trophies all arrived via the river.

Charles VIII had his Italian booty brought up the river: one hundred and thirty tapestries, 39 leather wall panels with scenes in gold, lengths of velvet and damasks, illuminated books, paintings and sculpture. The booty was accompanied by tailors, cabinetmakers, makers of organs, decorators, a maker of artificial incubators and even a parrot breeder.

The river too, and a project for the canal of Amboise, is how Francis I convinced Leonardo, who was already old, to follow him to

France with "La Gioconda", which he bought for 4,000 ducats. The grand old man lived in Clos-Lucé, in the residence prepared for him, in close touch with the king. Here he received frequent visits, the honor and the respect his fame inspired.

Besides canals, Leonardo designed automata which frightened the court ladies, fireworks and great public illuminations which concluded the days spent hunting in Amboise and Chambord.

The guests were ambassadors, important dignitaries and sovereigns. Among these was the Emperor Charles V, who considered the castle as a "summus" of human ingenuity.

Francis I.

A glimpse of court life in the XVI century may also be useful in understanding the period.

In 1539, when Charles V, emperor of Spain and Flanders, arrived in Chambord, the whole valley was in ferment.

Fêtes of all kinds, perhaps the most sumptuous ever planned, were in preparation.

Long rows of wagons, servants unloading enormous quantities of food: oysters and fish from the Atlantic, huge trophies of fruit, plumed wildfowl, quarters of deer, barrels of wine. Tables set with silver, roaring fires.

Walls lined with fabrics, the perfume of incense, lutes, guitars, torches held by pages, with light flickering on the fresh complexions and jewels of the ladies.

In the procession the king and the queen, young princesses and princes of Europe, were the dauphin Henry II and his young wife Catherine de' Medici, who learned the lesson well and later organized ceremonies that were grander and more ruinous.

The fêtes, the balls, the tournaments, were the culminating moment in the life of a court that also lived on intrigue: stories of repudiated wives, of ill-assorted marriages, of murders, courtesans and secret struggles for power. All set against the backdrop of

Catherine de' Medici.

the châteaux which become more and more beautiful.

Every residence, be it royal, noble, or bourgeois, has its stories of hidden life which will be discovered in the pages that follow. From the murder of the Duke of Guise to the perfidious play of jealousy between the great Catherine de' Medici and the equally powerful courtesan Diane de Poitiers, to whom Henry II had given, as a gift, one of the less spectacular but more amenable châteaux, Chenonceau, which at the death of the king returned

Chenonceau.

into the hands of the queen.

She installed herself in the castle with her "Escadron Volant" consisting of the youngest and loveliest ladies of France whose role was that of entertaining the palace guests.

The fêtes were no longer the fabulous and regal spectacles they once had been but now were a matter of play: disguises, verdant hiding places, a switching of roles.

Extravagances in which the lovely ladies of the "Escadron Volant" dressed (or undressed) as available Nymphs (as described by Brantôme) served sumptuous banquets in the shade of rockworks. Catherine's decadence and refinement was handed down and accentuated in the three kings she bore to Henry II – Francis II, Charles IX and above all Henry III, the most frivolous and immoral of the lot, who alternated between mystical crises and the most licentious entertainment which cost the treasury a fortune and his subjects exorbitant, crushing taxes.

Then came the religious wars, the night of St. Bartholomew (August 24, 1572), the plague which appeared more than once – in 1583, in 1584 and in 1586. In 1607 it decimated the population of Tours.

Dearth and famine followed. The fortunes of the nobles and the greater bourgeoisie melted away in their attempts to imitate the ostentation of the court. The valley was impoverished. The important silk industries languished, agriculture was degraded.

The decline of the valley coincided with the end of the house of Valois. The regal processions which wound their way through the valley from fêtes and entertainment in one dwelling to those in another kept on dwindling.

Palaces that were large, and stable, and monumental began to be appreciated.

The star of Fontainebleau waxed brighter.

The châteaux of the Loire had reached the end of their roles as leading actors, and they now stand as extraordinary witnesses of times gone by and gems of a glorious epoch.

Elsa Nofri Rosi

INDEX OF THE ITINERARIES

   The great chateaux

   Important chateaux

   Monuments and religious buildings

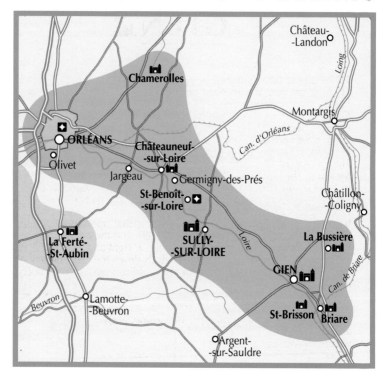

The elegant shape of the château of Gien, with its unmistakeable red brick façade, mirrored on the waters of the Loire.

GIEN

The city of Gien, situated in the valley of the Loire, which is rich in game, has always been an important center for hunting and has even earned the name of "Capital of the Hunt".

Game has always been abundant in the immense forests of Orléans (34,000 hectares) which skirt the Loire from Gien to the Beauce. Gien is the northeast gate of the Sologne and the Loire is a stopping place for migratory animals.

The château of Gien was an ideal location for the creation of a **Hunt Museum**. The building, whose story will be briefly related, was built in 1484 on the site of a royal hunting rendez-vous by Anne de Beaujeu, eldest daughter of Louis XI and Regent of France, who had received this Crown possession from the king.

It consists of a vast building with windows that open to the south, overlooking the city at its feet and the Loire and the countryside on the horizon. To the east another building, at right angles to the first, looks out on the river which lazily winds down towards the valley and as far as the horizon where the hills of Sancerre can just barely be distinguished.

The façades on the inner courtyard, less severe in their lines, are pleasingly embellished by three small octagonal towers in brick and stone with fine stone spiral staircases inside; above are square rooms, flanked again by round turrets which enclose narrower staircases.

When Anne de Beaujeu died, the castle returned to the Crown. Within these walls Francis I in 1523 signed the document which conferred the regency on Louise of Savoy. Henry II stayed here, as did Catherine de' Medici and Charles IX during the Religious Wars. Henry III and Anne of Austria lived here, and Louis XIV, who was then 13, sought refuge here during the battle of Bleneau in which the vis-

The Guard Room, with its splendid trussed ceiling, is part of the International Museum of the Hunt and contains numerous pictures by François Desportes (1661-1743), the official artist of the royal hunt.

count de Turenne came forth as victor. The château belonged in turn to various great families until the county of Gien was suppressed during the Revolution. In 1823 the château was acquired by the department of Loiret.

The collections are lively and instructive. Chronologically arranged, they tell the story of hunting throughout the centuries by means of hunter's weapons as well as drawings, etchings, paintings, tapestries, decorated ceramics and accessories.

There are flintlock guns with extremely long barrels to ensure a greater firing range and to make it possible to shoot from horseback without running the risk of hitting one's mount, as well as two-barrelled guns. These firearms, sculpted, engraved, damascened, inlaid with ivory, tortoise shell, mother-of-pearl or precious metals, are in themselves works of art.

The lovely room on the first floor contains more than 75 paintings and studies by François Desportes (1661-1743). Of all the rooms in the château this was the only one where this extraordinary collection could be suitably presented.

There is no doubt that Desportes was the greatest painter of animals France produced. He was assigned to the person of King Louis XIV and followed him when he went hunting, painting the finest game the king killed as well as portraits of his best dogs: Blanche Ponne, Zette, etc. Gifted with a unique skill, he worked with an untiring virtuosity. He executed large decorations for the royal and princely houses and large hunting scenes of all kinds.

It is particularly interesting to compare the projects or studies and the large finished paintings.

Two large canvases by J.B. Oudry (1686-1755), who was Desportes' successor as painter of the king's hunts, have been hung near the latter artist's paintings so that the two styles can be compared. In fact, for a long time Oudry was the better known of the two even though he seems never to have done anything comparable. An exception is the large "Wolf Hunt" in the Museum which, to experts, is one of the painter's best works.

In 1972 the Museum was presented with the exceptional collection of the personal trophies of Claude Hettier de Boislambert, Grand Chancellor of the Order of the Liberation and Honorary President of the International Hunting Council. Claude Hettier de Boislambert was primarily interested in protecting nature and animals. He was an exemplary hunter and conceived of hunting as rational exploitation and regulation of natural resources.

The 500 trophies on exhibition were collected in the course of 50 years of hunting as a sport. The animals to be killed were always carefully chosen and were always "approached" on foot.

An entire room is dedicated to a rare collection of 5,000 hunting buttons, small works of art created for the tunics of the supervisors of the royal hunts.

More than 50 hunting horns, set against a background of the colors of the royal hunt, trace the evolution of the horn from the time of Louis XIV to our days.

BRIARE

In 1890, in order to join two canals without flowing into the Loire, work began on constructing a canal-bridge, 664 metres long, to cross the river. Opened in 1897, this veritable work of art, made of stone and metallic structures, with the contribution of Gustave Eiffel, receives a one way navigable waterway, regularly used by boats and flanked by two paths reserved for pedestrians and cyclists.

ST-BRISSON ⛫

The castle of Saint-Brisson is located in the village of the same name, just a few kilometers south of Gien, on the left bank of the Loire. Originally it was a military fortress that was besieged by King Louis VI; King Philippe Auguste stayed there in 1181. The castle's layout dates from the XII century: it was a regular hexagon (part is missing today) of buildings, bounded by alternating square and round towers. The castle was considerably modified in the XVII and XIX centuries. The rooms, too, were drastically changed in the XIX and XX centuries. The castle gardens have an exhibition of reproductions of Medieval war machines.

LA BUSSIÈRE 🏯

The castle of La Bussière is located at the far end of the village of the same name, just a few kilometers east of Gien. In the XII century, Etienne de Feins built a fortress on what is now the site of the castle to defend himself from the Bourbons. The property was inherited by Etienne Fromond, Minister of Justice under Charles VII and first president of the parliament under Louis XII. In 1518, Jean du Tillet, chancellor of the Parliament of Paris inherited it, and the castle remained in his family for three centuries. It was a refuge for 15 priests of Gien during the wars of religion in 1567, but the besieged fortress fell, and the priests were beheaded by the Huguenot troops and the castle was severely damaged. In the XVI century the Tillet family began building a more tranquil residence (with outbuildings, double circle of walls, and drawbridge). Jean-Baptiste du Tillet, a member of Louis XIV's court, commissioned Le Nôtre to design the gardens, he also built two pavilions at the gate and a monumental gate. After the Revolution the castle was sold to the administrator of the Tillet estates, then to a wood merchant who then sold it to the count of Chasseval, ancestor of the current owners. The main building is made of brick and stone, with a slate roof; its entrance tower dates from the XVI century, and nearly the entire structure was rebuilt at the beginning of the XVIII century and restored with a heavy hand in the XIX. The noteworthy annexes in the courtyard date from the XVII century.

One can admire the XVI century spiral staircase, a Venetian veranda (XIX century) that offers a lovely view of the pond, and the interesting **Musée de la pêche** (fishing museum) in one of the rooms that was remodelled in the XIX century.

SULLY-SUR-LOIRE

At the entrance to the village of Sully-sur-Loire stands a Medieval looking castle, that seems to rise out of the water and surrounded by towers.

In the XIV century Guy de la Trémoïlle, a favorite of King Charles V, built the rectangular donjon with four square towers and a door with two smaller towers to the south. The building was designed by the king's architect Raymond du Temple. The "small castle" was built in the mid-fifteenth century: it encloses the courtyard south of the rectangular donjon, and comprises a house and two towers that herald the Renaissance. In 1602 Maximilien de Béthune, King Henry IV's famous finance minister, better known as Sully, acquired the property. He built a tower in 1605 and had the interior remodelled. The castle belonged to his descendants until 1962. In the XVIII century, another building was added to the donjon and the "small castle"; this part was entirely rebuilt after the fire of 1918.

In addition to Guy de la Trémoïlle and Sully, the castle also hosted Joan of Arc, Charles VII, Voltaire and the Marquis de La Fayette. After the death of King Henry IV, Sully wrote his "Mémoires des sages et royales économies d'État de Henri le Grand". Voltaire used the great hall of honor for performances of "Artémises", and it was at the castle that he wrote "Henriade".

On foot, the castle is reached by crossing two bridges that provide an excellent view of the whole complex. In the courtyard there is a donjon built by King Philippe Auguste, and a statue of Sully. The gardens, of which only a large area surrounded by canals remains, bear witness to the major work Sully had done in the XVII century in order to protect the castle from being flooded by the Loire River. Inside one can admire the magnificent 300 square metre main hall

with its 7 metre ceilings, the reconstructed king's bedroom, the duke's bedroom in the Renaissance pavilion and the splendid Gothic oak ceiling (late XIV century), in the upper room of the Donjon, shaped like an overturned keel.

A famous classical music festival is held at the castle every year in June and July.

ST-BENOÎT▸

The Abbey of St-Benoît-de-Fleury, founded to receive the remains of St. Benedict, enjoyed particular fortune in the Carolingian period, under the abbot Theodulphus. The massive arcaded tower (early XI century), built high up to avoid flooding, with its cross-shaped pillars and beautiful storiated capitals; and the choir (1067-1080), rising above the crypt and surrounded by four chapels, constitute the oldest part of the Abbey.

The austere and luminous nave was, in fact, rebuilt in the XIII century and probably finished in 1218. It marks the ascendancy of the new Gothic art over the elegant and linear Romanesque structures of which the Abbey of St-Benoît still offers a splendid example.

The Abbey, a view of the nave.

The arcaded tower giving access to the abbey, with a detail of the columns and storiated capitals.

CHÂTEAUNEUF-SUR-LOIRE 🏰

T he early castles were the homes of feudal lords who often hosted kings in need of a rest: Philip I, Louis VI The Fat, Philippe
Auguste II, St-Louis, and Philip the Fair. In 1328 Charles IV also
called Charles Le Bel, meaning the Fair, died at Châteauneuf without any male heirs, thus ending the Capetian dynasty. Today, not a
trace remains of these buildings. During the Hundred Years' War
the palace became a formidable citadel for the Dukes of Orléans
(crenelated towers, war machines, portcullises, etc.). John II the
Good and Edward III of England met there after the Treaty of
Brétigny. On June 22 1429 Joan of Arc met Charles VII there before
his coronation at Reims. In 1562 Coligny and the Prince of Condé
took possession of Châteauneuf. Henry of Navarre entrusted Marshal Daumont to defend the city; the wars of religion led to the
destruction of the castle which was rebuilt in the XVII century. After
six centuries of ownership the Crown sold the castle in 1646 to
Michel Particelli, advisor to king Louis XIV and superintendent of
Finances. In 1653, Louis Phelypeaux, secretary of state to Louis XIV
became the new owner. He had Lefebvre build a new castle, with
luxuriant gardens designed by Le Nôtre. It was a "small Versailles"
with an extraordinary bathhouse. In 1783 the castle was purchased
by the Duke of Penthièvre, grandson of Louis XIV and Madame de
Montespan. He enlarged and beautifed the castle: the courtyard,
four pavilions, the iron gate, the conservatory and the Galerie de la
Rotonde were added. During the Revolution the castle and gardens

*Châteauneuf-sur-Loire: a partial view of the
classic-style domed rotonda.*

were devastated. The remains of the castle were purchased by Lebrun who ordered the main building destroyed. The gardens reverted to fields. In the XIX century Madame Ladureau, Lebrun's daughter commissioned Huillard d'Hérou to build an English garden (with exotic trees, 430 different species rhododendrons, etc.). Today, all that remains are the domed XVIII century rotonda (which is the town hall), the pavilions of the first courtyard, and interesting outbuildings and stables built by Mansart. The western part of the gardens is bounded by filled moats, crossed by a picturesque stone bridge. The castle is actually located in the heart of the town. Some rooms on the ground floor of the rotonda house the well-documented **Musée de la Marine de Loire** (Loire shipping museum).

CHAMEROLLES

The château of Chamerolles was built in 1522, according to the wishes of Lancelot du Lac, governor of Orléans. Situated on the threshold of the forest of Orléans, the château has the appearance of a vast stone and brick quadrilateral, consisting of three wings marked at the corners by four towers. To the east, the large courtyard is open on the side of the access tower, flanked by four small cylindrical towers. The château is surrounded by a large park, the gardens of which have recently been returned to their former splendour and opened to the public.

ORLÉANS:

This beautiful and interesting city, with its many historical, architectural and artistic monuments is set in a graceful position the right bank of the Loire River. It is the capital of the Centre region. It has both a busy industrial section and a flourishing rural economy based on nurseries and vineyards. It has been written that "if Paris is the head of France, Orléans is its heart". Originally called *Cenabum* by the Gauls, it was Romanized by Caesar's legions in 52 B.C. Under its new name of *Aurelianis*, it survived a siege by the Huns, and was a longtime residence of the Capetians (X-XI centuries). But the city's fame is linked to the important events that occured during the Hundred Year's War when Joan of Arc, now the patron saint of France, freed the city from the English siege with an army provided by the dauphin, the future King Charles VII (on 8

The Cathédrale Ste-Croix.

May 1429) and earned the title of the "Maid of Orléans".

A salient feature in an interesting town, and outstanding part of the scenery is the **Cathédrale Ste-Croix**: this grandiose building is an exemplary model of the French Gothic. Even though the building's origins date from the XIII century, its current appearance is the result of reconstruction that was begun in the XVII century and lasted well into the XIX, following almost total destruction by Protestants in 1568.

The highly ornate façade with three grandiose portals, each

The Cathédrale Ste-Croix, a view of the nave.

Joan of Arc

Born into a peasant family in 1412 at Domrémy, in the Vosges district, at the tender age of 13 Joan began hearing miraculous "voices" (the Archangel Michael, Saint Margaret, Saint Catherine), that induced her to undertake a divine mission: that of freeing France from English rule and reinstalling Charles VI, who had ceded the throne to Henry V of England in 1420. With great determination, the girl met with Charles and persuaded him of her mission; then, in 1429, at the head of a squad of soldiers, she liberated Orléans, under siege by the English, and earned for herself the name of "Maid of Orléans."

Nor did she stop here: when she had conquered Beaugency and defeated the English at Patay, she liberated the Loire region, thus permitting Charles VII to enter Reims and to be crowned king of France on 17 July 1429. The dream had come true, but Joan's sad fate was decreed: opposed at court due to her ascendency over the king, and worn down by defeats in a number of battles, she was captured near Compiègne on 24 May 1430 by the Burgundians, who turned her over to the English. She was taken to Rouen, where she was tried for heresy by a court of the Inquisition. She attempted to defend her cause, but in vain: on 30 May 1431 she was burned at the stake. Today Joan of Arc, sainted in 1920, is the patron saint of France.

topped by rose windows is embellished with ediculae and crowned by an elegant loggia with ogival arches and lavish fretwork. Two graceful soaring twin towers (XVIII century) repropose typical French Gothic themes. The big statues on the façade portray the Evangelists.

A steep, pointed spire rises from the nave. The monumental interior has five naves. The severe central nave is topped with ribbed ogival cross vaults. The most interesting elements include the XVIII century woodcarvings on the choir, by Degoullons who had previously worked in Paris and at Versailles and an early XVII century marble statue of the Madonna carved by M. Bourdin, a local sculptor; the statue stands in the chapel located at the center of the apse. The Chapel of Joan of Arc, to the left of the choir has a statue of Cardinal Touchet, the champion of the cult of the "Maid", who lived in the late XIX-early XX century. The Crypt contains vestiges of three ancient houses of worship that existed between the IV and X centuries, and the tombs of bishops who lived between the XIII and XIV centuries with many interesting artifacts that are now displayed in the Treasure Room Not far from the cathedral is the old graveyard that was originally outside the XII century walls that enclosed the Medieval city. Today it is more of a rectangular garden enclosed by sixteenth century porticoes.

The **Musée des Beaux-Arts** has many fine art works. On the second floor it is important to see the "Virgin and Child with Angels" by Matteo di Giovanni (Sienese school, XV century); a marble statue portraying the "Virgin and Child" (XIV century); and works by Italian, Flemish and Dutch artists such as Tintoretto, Correggio, Annibale Carracci, Van der Velde, Van Goyen, Pourbus, Velazquez. The paintings on the first floor are by French masters from the XVII and XVIII centuries: C. Vignon, Ph. de Champaigne, Louis le Nain, C.

*These pages,
two partial views of the
classical urban architecture.*

Deruet. The outstanding XVIII century portraitists include F. Hubert Drouais, L. Tocqué, J.B. Perronneau. Paintings by Courbet, Gauguin, Rouault, and Max Jacob and statuary complete the group of works by XIX-XX century artists.

The elegant Hotel Cabu (XVI century) is now the home of the **Musée Historique** (Historical Museum). One of its greatest masterpieces is the Gallic-Roman Treasure from Neuvy-en-Sullias. The **House of Joan of Arc** overlooking the central Place du Général de Gaulle, is the reconstruction of where the French national heroine stayed. Mementoes, audiovisual presentations and various artifacts help retell her epic story.

Other highlights at Orléans include the central, porticoed Rue Royale that leads to the panoramic **Pont George V**, the Hotel Groslot, a lovely, XVI century Renaissance house, and the churches of **St-Pierre-le-Puellier** (XII century, Romanesque) and **St-Aignan** (Gothic, consecreated in 1509).

FROM ORLÉANS TO BLOIS

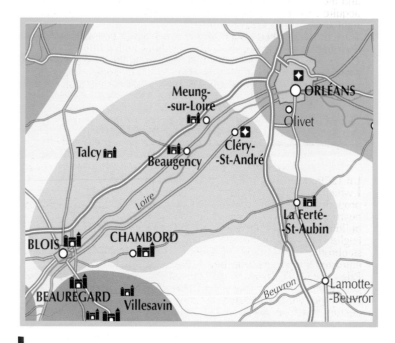

LA FERTÉ-ST-AUBIN 🏛

The castle of La Ferté-St-Aubin stands on the banks of the Cosson, near the old part of the village where one can still admire some traditional, woodframed, brick houses of Sologne.

Between 1590 and 1620 Henri de St-Nectaire built the existing left portion of the main building over the ruins of a castle that had been destroyed in 1562. Between 1630 and 1640 his son, Henri II de la Ferté-Sennecterre, Marshal of France, continued the construction and built the right por-

tion of the main building as well as the stables (adjacent to the left) and the left pavilion. In 1746, the Marshal of France de Lowendal acquired La Ferté and built the right pavilion, the annexes on the right and a neo-Gothic chapel.

The castle is reached via a bridge, through a monumental, old-style door framed by two domed-roofed pavilions with a round window. The architecturally noteworthy buildings are in the style of François Mansart. The castle is built of brick and rows of stone in a pleasant color. An interesting **Museum of Horses** concludes the tour.

CLÉRY ST-ANDRÉ ▪

In 1280, near Cléry, a statue of the Madonna, which soon proved to have miraculous properties, was found and placed in a chapel nearby. In its honour, Philip the Fair had a building erected which was destroyed by the English in 1428. Charles of Orléans and his stepbrother, the Count of Dunois, who entrusted the project to architects Pierre Le Paige and Pierre Chauvin, and Louis XI who, in order to fulfil a vow gave great impetus to the completion of the work, are responsible for the present Notre-Dame de Cléry, finished at the end of the XV century to which, between 1515 and 1521, another three chapels were added. One of the chapels, dedicated to St. James, recalls the fact that St. James of Compostela often passed through Cléry on his pilgrimages. Thanks to complex restoration work, the church has reached the present day in all its splendour, having survived the devastation caused by the Huguenots in 1562 and 1567. Louis XI and his consort, Charlotte of Savoy, rest here, and their sepulchral marble monument, by Michel Bourdin (1622), dominates the left side of the nave; their son, Charles VIII also rests here as does the Count of Dunois, in the Longueville chapel he had built for himself and his descendants, in the middle of the XV century, by the architect Colin du Val.

The tombstone of Charles VIII.

The sober elegance of the façade of Notre-Dame de Cléry.

MEUNG-SUR-LOIRE🏰

The castle of Meung-sur-Loire stands in the middle of the village, on a hillside on the banks of the Loire.
Originally, there stood a XI century Medieval castle that had been besieged by Louis VI the Fat, in 1101. Several generations of the Meung family lived in this castle. The last, Jehan de Meung was one of the authors of the "Roman de la Rose". From the XII to the XVIII century the castle was the official residence of the bishops of Orléans. In the XII century Manassès de Garlande, bishop of Orléans ordered the building of the Manassès tower (adjacent to the collegiate church of St-Liphard). In 1361 the castle was occupied by the Anglo-Navarrese (Hugues de Calverly). In the XV century during the Hundred Years' War, the English conquered it. On June 14, 1429, Joan of Arc attacked the city, and General Talbot fled. In the XV century the poet François Villon was imprisoned in the dungeons. Condemned to death, he wrote his "Grand Testament" before being pardoned by King Louis XI who visited Meung. In the XVII century the castle was abandoned and fell into ruin. In the XVII century, King Louis XIV offered the sum of 20,000 francs to Monsignor Fléuriau d'Amenonville who had some important work done. An annex was erected on the south side; the old towers and original building were not modified. In 1791 the castle was sold at auction to J.J. Lecoulfeux who later founded the Banque de France and became Mayor of Meung.
The impressive entrance façade which still shows some signs of the drawbridge dates from feudal times. The façade of the main entran-

ce was opened in the XVI century, remodelled in the XVIII century and then covered with a surprising coat of pink plaster. The interior of the castle was greatly modified during the XIX century. One can tour the twenty-one rooms that are furnished in the most varied styles: Louis XIII bedroom, Louis XV furniture, Spanish dining-room and a curious XVIII century bathroom with accessories, etc. In the underground rooms one can see some cells, and a surprising XII century chapel with palm vaulting.

The remains of the Manassès tower, close to the college of St-Liphard.

BEAUGENCY

B eaugency is a village between Beauce and Sologne, on the banks of the Loire. It is delightful to stroll along its typical streets flanked by an important group of civil and religious buildings erected between the XI and XVIII centuries (church of Notre-Dame where two councils were held, the tower of St-Firmin, the Clock tower, the César tower, the Château Dunois, the house of the Templars, the town hall, the Tavers gate, the bridge over the Loire that offers a beautiful view, etc.).

On the site of the castle of the lords of Beaugency, that was built in the XI century, the bastard of Orléans (illegitimate son of the Duke of Orléans Louis I and Marietta d'Enghien), and nephew of Charles VI, step-brother to Charles d'Orléans, built the castle after he became lord of Beaugency upon his marriage to Marie d'Harcourt. Jean, bastard of Orléans, a soldier, comrade of Joan of Arc who defended Orléans and freed Montargis, lived in the castle from 1440 to 1457, that is, until he moved to Châteaudun. The castle belonged to the Dunois-Longueville family until 1789. Initially it was abandoned, then converted into a hospice for the poor and later into a regional holiday camp; now the castle is the **Regional Museum of Crafts and Traditions of the Orléans District**. It houses various collections (furniture, clothing and headresses, tools, toys, engravings, interior scenes, etc.) that illustrate the customs of the region. The museum also contains mementos of the writer Eugène Sue.

The sturdy XI century bastion next to the château.

The composite façade of the church of Notre-Dame.

The **Château Dunois** located in the historical town center, next to the César tower is a fine example of XI century military architecture (in this period the donjons were rectangular and supported by buttresses). The original five stories are in ruins. The Château Dunois is a typical XVI century residence with double-light windows, stepped towers and towers with arches. The rooms have undergone major changes in the past two hundred years and only the garrets are in the original state.

The church of Notre-Dame, a view of the nave.

TALCY

The castle of Talcy is located in the middle of a charming village of Beauce, a few kilometers from Mer.

In 1517 Bernardo Salviati, a Florentine banker, member of the court of King Francis I and a relative of the powerful Medici family, purchased the Talcy estate with "house, dovecot and annexes". In 1520 he received permission to make Talcy over into a "fortress-house". He added traditional feudal elements without, however, fortifying it: this makes the building an architectural archaism. In the XVII century Isabelle, daughter of Scipione Sardini was the last of the Salviati line. Ownership passed to the Godet des Marais family. In the XVIII century Jérémie Burgeat, advisor to the Parliament of Metz, rebuilt the roofs, floors, windows, wooden fittings, doors and restored the rooms. In 1780 Talcy was purchased by Gastebois, ancestor of the last owner, Mademoiselle Stapfer, member of a Swiss banking family. In 1932 ownership was transferred to the French government.

Cassandra, Bernardo Salviati's daughter lived in the castle; she was the first love of Ronsard ("Les amours"). Her daughter was an ancestor of the poet Alfred de Musset. In 1562 the Talcy Conference brought Catherine de' Medici, Charles IX and the Prince of Condé, emissary of the leaders of the Reformation together at the castle.

One enters the castle through a beautiful door comprising a massive XV century tower with polygonal corner towers in brick and stone. There are neither drawbridges nor moats. The original windows were modified in the XVIII century. The façade of the main building (east) is extremely fascinating. The projecting wing was remodelled in the XVIII century. Note the square loopholes bordered with redans. A graceful Italian-style well decorates the first courtyard. The remarkably well-preserved XVI century dovecot with 1500 compartments is in the second courtyard. One of the outbuildings has a still-functional, four hundred year old press. The rooms were remodelled for the last time in the XVIII century. They are very charming and contain fine XVI-XVIII century furniture

as well as Gothic tapestries. The large garden with orchards and vegetable patches is is also interesting. At the southern end of the village one can visit an old wooden windmill.

The vicinity of Talcy provides some pleasant sights: an old wooden windmill (top) and vast cultivated fields, with their incomparable shades of colour.

CHAMBORD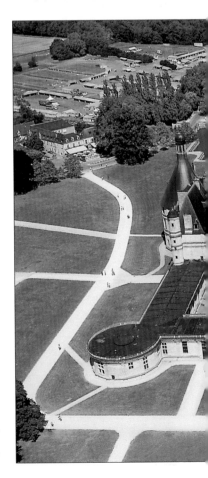

The château of Chambord is one of the loveliest Renaissance buildings in the valley of the Loire. The land on which it stands was the property of the Counts of Blois, of Champagne and of Chatillon from the X century on, until it was bought by Louis d'Orléans in 1392. When the new Duke of Orléans became king (as Louis XII) the county became the property of the crown. This elegant château was built by Francis I, Louis XII's successor, who came to the throne in 1515 when he was only 20 years old. Francis I, who was the son of Louise of Savoy, had been particularly impressed by the figure of Lorenzo the Magnificent, an outstanding personality in the field of politics and culture.

The conquest of the territory of Milan provided Francis I with the opportunity of seeing the architecture of northern Italy. As a great patron of the arts and sciences, he succeeded in bringing Leonardo da Vinci to France. The king's wish to fuse the elements of Italian Renaissance architecture with those of the French tradition in a single building was partially granted when the château of Blois was enlarged. Leonardo da Vinci worked there too, in 1517, on a project for a castle that was never built. In 1519 he died in Clos-Lucé, near Amboise, it is said in the arms of Francis I who had hastened to his bedside.

It was in that year that work on the large building which was to become the king's country residence and hunting reserve was begun on the estate of Chambord on the site of an older stronghold which had been demolished to make room for the new castle. All of 1800 men worked on the château and its additions from 1526 on. The archives offer us no information as to the name of the architect, but an analysis of the structures reveals a profound influence of Leonardo's thought and an extremely close tie to some of

Francis I.

the projects by Domenico da Cortona. While in France under Charles VIII, Domenico had executed a wooden model of a castle with a square keep and large rooms on a cross plan which divided each floor into four sectors with identical

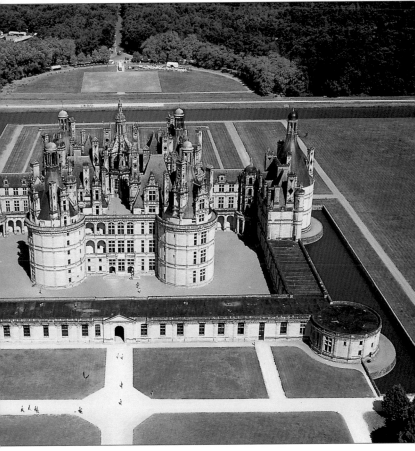

apartments. One of the arms of the cross was, in the plan, taken up by straight flights of stairs which led from one floor to the next. The central keep of the château of Chambord fully respects this model and is thus related to Italian architecture and of classical inspiration. The cross plan had in fact been abandoned in antiquity, and only the basilica of St. Peter's in Rome, by Bramante in 1507, had used it. The division of the floors into apartments that are separate but alike reveals the strong influence of contemporary Tuscan villas, while the large terraces and the magnificent spiral staircase at the center of the cross bear Leonardo's mark. Although this type of staircase is derived from the Medieval concept, it goes far beyond it in its unique division into two separate flights with numerous openings on the arms of the corridors. A tribute to the former Medieval French tradition is to be found in the presence of powerful cylindrical towers at the corners of the keep, which however harmonize with the building.

Construction work continued for years. Around 1537 the keep was finished, in 1540 the two floors of the wing with the royal apartments were built, together with the ground floor of the wing with the chapel and the walls of the annexes; while it was not until 1547, when Francis I died, that the wing of the royal apartments was completed.

The keep, seat of the royal court, had rooms arranged in a cross plan on each of its three floors and it was here that the social life of the courtiers took place. Balls were held on the second floor, where the ceilings of the rooms were enriched with coffering and vaulting. In the sectors marked off by the arms of the cross there were four apartments per floor, in addition to another four in the corner tow-

Two evocative images of the château, a true masterpiece of the French Renaissance, with details of the terrace and elaborate roofing.

ers. As said before, each apartment was just like the others: composed of a large hall as high as the whole floor and of two rooms, a study and a wardrobe, above which were rooms for service. Almost all the rooms (365 out of 440) had a fireplace so that each apartment could be independently heated. The double spiral staircase in the center, topped by a lantern, connected the various floors up to the top of the castle. The staircase is related to a project by Leonardo for a spiral staircase which consisted of four distinct superimposed flights of stairs, in other words just as many stairs as quarters and arms of the cross in the castle. It is therefore likely that Leonardo da Vinci's staircase, which may have been conceived for Chambord, was then simplified when it was built by the master masons of the building yard.

The top of the stairs leads to the large terraces of the castle, which again correspond to one of Leonardo's ideas, in which he intended them to be used as a place from which to admire the superstructures of the buildings. Along the walks which follow the cross plan, or those which skirt the perimeter of the wings and the towers, the members of the court could take walks and retire to observe the surrounding countryside and the hunts that were held there, as well as the decorations of the castle roof. As can be seen even from a distance, the upper part of the keep is crowded with dormer windows with Italianate classicizing superstructures, small towers, pavilions and elegant chimneys decorated with columns, clouds, miniature pediments, salamanders and geometric motifs in slate, applied to create a two-color effect similar to that of the Italian monuments in polychrome marble. The upper part of the lantern, which lies above the spiral staircase rises 32 metres up into the air. Originally open – the glass was added later – the upper part is supported by projecting round-headed arches of Medieval origin. The sculpture inside the keep, executed between 1525 and 1550, displays the profound influence of Italian classical art.

The large central double spiral staircase supported by four pillars culminating in a skylight.

A ceramic masterpiece with the coat of arms of Marshal Maurice de Saxe (XVIII c.)

A floor plan such as that of the keep which provided for apartments that were all alike was not suitable for the royal apartments, which had to be larger and more sumptuous. With this in mind the two wings for the king's rooms and for the chapel were added in 1526. Although they could obviously not have been foreseen in the original plan, the new parts seem an integral part of the keep in their style, concept and proportions. In fact these later wings used the side of the keep as the unit of measure: it was multiplied by three and by two respectively for the width and depth of the new buildings. The royal apartments, situated in the northeast corner and in part conceived like the others, had two extra rooms. One, which was very large and long, was the official audience hall, illuminated by rows of windows like some of the rooms in the palace of Fontainebleau. The other room, more intimate and reached by means of a staircase, was a private study in Italian Renaissance style. There were two walls with windows and a coffered ceiling decorated with carvings of salamanders and the initial F of Francis I.

The chapel, situated to the northwest, was also profoundly influenced by Italian art and through this, by classic art: double Doric columns and pediments are combined with a large barrel vault (which in the original project had the usual coffering). The plan of the castle, in its absolute symmetry, can be symbolically interpreted: the keep, seat of the court with standardized apartments, is set between the wing of Francis I and that of the chapel; that is, between the king and God. Other theories, based on the observation of the park, go even further and interpret the large trees in the woods as a symbol of the people and the circular enclosing walls of the estate, 33 kilometers long, as the symbol of the French boundaries.

A detail of the vaulted ceiling of the Guardroom, with the initials and symbol - the salamander - of Francis I.

The life and activity within the castle took place principally in the rooms in the arms of the cross and on the staircases. In moving from one floor to another and from one apartment to another the courtiers used the central staircase and the rooms as well as the loggias which lead to the corner towers. It was also possible to use the spiral staircases which cut through the thickness of the corner towers and put the floors and the landings of the apartments in communication and in addition led to the bathrooms on the ground floor in moving about between the floors. Francis I, together with his wife Eleanor, his mistress Anne de Pisseleu and the court, resided off and on in Chambord. Besides various official encounters, the king usually went there for a few weeks every two years for hunting. On the other hand, in addition to his many official obligations, he had many other hunting lodges to choose from. The considerable quantity of furnishings he brought in his wake remained in the castle only as long as the king was there. Among these were trunks, chests, bunk beds and wall hangings, including many tapestries which decorated the walls and made the rooms warmer.

In the winter of 1539, when Charles V came to stay in the castle, the Baron of Montmorency (grand master of ceremonies) installed a particularly luxuriant interior decoration. The emperor, who it is said was preceded by maidens who threw flower petals in his path, admired the castle and defined it, together with the objects it contained, "a synthesis of what human industry can accomplish". Francis I, who was a connoisseur of women, included 27 young ladies of rank in his household and many more in that of the queen. Indeed, he said "a court without women is like a year without spring and a spring without roses". Even so, in the autumn of 1545 the melancholy king wrote the words "woman is fickle, unhappy he who trusts her" on a window pane with his diamond ring.

The monumental bed in the bedroom of Louis XIV.

The hunting room of Francis I, the queen's bedroom and the dauphine Marie Antoinette.

When Francis I died the royal residence moved to Paris. His son and successor Henry II however continued work on Chambord, realizing the second floor of the chapel and all those structures decorated with a sculptured H, his emblem. In 1552 the treaty which united the three bishoprics of Toul, Metz and Verdun, which he had previously occupied, was signed here. On his death in 1559 work on the castle stopped, although Catherine de' Medici continued to frequent the palace together with her children. Charles IX was particularly fond of hunting and many tales are told about his prowess as a hunter and a rider. It is said that he was able to follow a deer until it was exhausted without using his dogs.

After his death in 1574 the castle was practically unused for about fifty years, since Henry III and Henry IV rarely stopped there. In 1626 Louis XIII gave his brother Gaston d'Orléans the county of Blois which included the château of Chambord. Actually this gift seems not to have been dictated so much by motives of brotherly love as by the desire to free himself of doubts as to Gaston's loyalty. The new owner immediately began to repair the residence. The tale is told of how in playing with his daughter, of whom he was particularly fond, Gaston d'Orléans agreed to climb up and down one of the flights of the large spiral staircase while his daughter ran up and down the other without ever meeting him.

Later the château once again became part of the property of the crown and Louis XIV, even though he stayed there only nine times, began important works of restoration and transformation. He abandoned Francis I's original royal wing and moved into new apartments remodelled for him in the front of the castle. New rooms on the first floor and luxurious furnishings arrived to enrich the castle from 1680 on, together with the addition of a new entrance with a pediment. The estate itself, which up to then had been covered with natural vegetation, was in part redeveloped into parks.

In 1669 Molière and Lulli wrote "Monsieur de Pourceaugnac" here and it was first presented privately for the king. It is recalled that because the leading actor was indisposed Lulli himself agreed to replace him at the last moment so as not to deprive the king of the show. Despite the fact that Lulli acted well and that there were plenty of comic situations, he noticed that Louis XIV was not laughing. Not even the lively scene of the druggists succeeded in getting the king to smile. At this point, improvising, Lulli quickly jumped off the stage, got a running start and landed with both feet on the harpsichord, smashing it to smithereens with a great racket. At this comic situation the king burst out laughing, clapping and decreeing the success of the play. The next year another work by Molière, "Le Bourgeois Gentilhomme" was presented in the castle. It is said that around this time, here in the castle, Anne Marie Louise d'Orleans declared her love to the Duc de Lauzun by writing the name of her beloved on a mirror after having clouded the surface with her breath.

Louis XIV's new preoccupations, above all the war, put a halt to the work. It was later carried on by Stanislao Leszczynski, to whom the

A beautiful "Polish style" bed, with its vivid tapestries, in the apartments refurbished in 1785 for the Marquis of Polignac.

manor had been given by his son-in-law Louis XV in 1725. Twenty years later the castle became the property of Marshal de Saxe, the victor of Prague, Fontenoy, Rocourt and Lawfeld. The king explicitly requested that the volunteers of De Saxe's regiment be quartered in the castle. These included Poles, Hungarians, Turks and Tartars in flashy uniforms as well as the "colonel company" of negros from Martinique mounted on white Ucrainian horses. In 1750 Marshal de Saxe mysteriously died. It is said that it was not pneumonia but rather that he fell in a duel with the Prince of Conti because of the latter's wife. After his death the castle cannons were fired every quarter of an hour for six days as a sign of mourning.

After having passed through other hands, the château risked being demolished after the Revolution, and in 1793 the fur-

Charles X, portrait kept in the gallery of the château.

The interior of the chapel, completed for Louis XIV by Jules Hardouin-Mansart.

Some of the portraits kept in the gallery of the château:
Louis XIII.

Henry IV.

nishings were dispersed. The castle continued to be in a critical state under Napoleon's empire when it belonged to Marshal Berthier and successively to the Duke of Bordeaux. During a visit, Gustave Flaubert wrote particularly haunting lines at the sight of the empty rooms "where the spider weaves its web on the salamander of Francis I".

Despite various attempts at restoration, such as the restoration of the lantern and all the beams, the building continued in its precarious state until 1947, when the State began restorations which were to continue for thirty years and which have not yet been completed.

Louis XIV.

The rooms of the château open to the public today contain various furnishings, including tapestries in the rooms of Louis XIV, and paintings, including the portraits of Henry III and Anne of Austria; other rooms contain objects which belonged to the Duke of Bordeaux, the Count of Chambord and last legitimate claimant to the throne of France. These include a bed and a toy battery of cannons in miniature. The ground floor contains an exhibit of the carriages built by Hermès in 1871 and which were never used. They were to have served the Count of Chambord in making his entrance into the capital to accede to the throne.

Louis XV.

Françoise d'Aubigné.

BLOIS.

This regal city on the Loire is rich in monuments, history and culture. It was the birthplace of Louis XII (1462), Denis Papin, who first conceived of the steam engine (1647), and J.N. Augustin Thierry, French Historian (1795).

Built in the XVI century, but destroyed by a hurricane in 1678 the **Cathédrale St-Louis** was reconstructed in the Gothic style towards the end of the XVII century. It is flanked by a tall Renaissance tower with a domed top. The crypt dates from the X-XI centuries.

The **St-Nicolas Church** was built between the XII and XIII centuries. The building is considered one of the finest blends of Romanesque and Gothic architecture.

Blois spreads along the banks of the Loire, with its
characteristic streets, typical houses and the Gothic
church of St-Nicolas, with its slender nave (below).

The Château of Blois

Even thousands of years ago the exceptional lie of the land around Blois was well-known – a rocky promontory hollowed out by the junction of the Loire and by a stream, easy to isolate and defend. It was no doubt used as early as the Neolithic Age, even though the existence of the castle was not documented until the IX century.

Towards the middle of the X century, Blois and the surrounding countryside were given in fief to very powerful noblemen, the Counts of Blois, vassals of the King of France and also counts of Tours, Chartres and later of Champagne: they rebuilt the fortified castle several times. The only remaining evidence of the imposing fortress built during the XIII century are a corner tower, fragments of ramparts and towers incorporated here and there in later constructions; and above all, the large assembly room and ballroom of the Counts of Blois.

At the end of the XIV century, the county of Blois was sold to Prince Louis of Orléans, son of the King of France Charles V, initiating a brilliant future for the town. His son, the poet Charles of Orléans, lived in the castle for 25 years after his return from serving a long prison sentence in England, attracting a small court of scholars and poets around him. But of even greater importance for the town, his grandson became King of France in 1498 under the name of Louis XII, following the accidental death in Amboise of his cousin, the

The famous Loggia façade, on the Francis I wing.

young Charles VIII, who died leaving no heirs. Born in Blois, Louis XII decided to fix his residence there. In this way, the small town of Blois became the royal town and capital of the kingdom during part of the XVI century. It was a very fortunate choice, as the town and region were rapidly expanding at the time and all their inhabitants were devoted to the Dukes of Orléans who had brought them so much prosperity.

At the time of Charles of Orléans, and especially under Louis XII and Francis I, the town of Blois grew considerably. But after the death of Queen Claude of France in 1524 and the disaster of Pavia in 1525, Francis I never returned to Blois and his successors only paid short visits to the town.

During the XVII century, the city was brought back to life by the prolonged stay (1634-1660) of Gaston d'Orléans, brother of Louis XIII. The kings paid little attention to the château of Blois throughout the XVIII century. It was divided into small apartments and used to house old servants of the Crown. The gardens were parcelled out and it fell into a state of general neglect. In 1788, Louis XVI ordered the sale of the castle or failing that, its demolition. It was saved by its transformation into a military barracks.

During and after the Revolution, various monuments of Blois were mutilated, or even destroyed stone by stone. The castle did not

The typically Gothic-shaped equestrian statue of the King in the internal courtyard of the Louis XII wing.

The symbols of the King and Queen Claude of France, sculptured on the fireplace in a first floor room: the salamander and the ermine.

escape these acts of vandalism and all the emblems and effigies of the royal family were effaced. During the first half of the XIX century, the castle was modified due to military occupation.

In 1845 the architect Duban began a radical restoration of the château which is now considered to have been excessive.

Louis XII wing. In 1498, Louis Duke of Orléans and Count of Blois became King of France under the name of Louis XII. The new king soon undertook to rebuild his ancestors' castle. The Louis XII wing, which originally extended on three sides of the court, was built rapidly in the space of three years. The new appearance of this gracious manor built in brick and stone is surprising. It is devoid of the towers and battlements which were still widespread during that period and the large windows, balconies, skylights and open galleries let in a great deal of air and light. The architecture of Louis XII's wing is serene, gay and gracious, in keeping with a king who was known for his simple, affable manner. It was no longer a fortified castle because Louis XII did not need to defend himself; his power was undisputed. By that stage, the King of France required a castle of government which could be used for receptions and balls. The king introduced a new way of governing, an "open" diplomacy inspired by the Italians, as can be seen

from the revolutionary diplomatic act that was the sumptuous reception held in 1501 in the castle of Blois in honour of the Archduke of Austria with whom France was practically at war.

If Louis XII's constructions were modern in design, they remained basically Gothic in many aspects: lack of regularity and symmetry in their plan and distribution of openings; fine, sharp-pointed, hollowed-out mouldings and rich, sculpted decorations, consisting, as in the cathedrals, of friezes of foliage, pinnacles and rosettes and in particular, of corbels with picturesque personages in a very Medieval vein.

According to French and Gothic tradition, the initials and emblems of the owners of the place are sculpted in the stone: fleur-de-lis for the king and ermine spots for the queen, Anne de Bretagne, on the columns of the gallery; porcupines, emblems of the Dukes of Orléans, on the Great Staircase ("De près comme de loin, je suis redoutable!"). An equestrian statue of the king crowns the main entrance of the château.

The gallery set against the chapel of which the southern half was destroyed during the XIX century was for many years wrongfully attributed to Charles of Orléans when it really was one of Louis XII's constructions. The greater restraint of this building is not at all surprising as it was a simple corridor connecting two main buildings and not a residential wing.

The existing chapel is the choir of the chapel built by Louis XII and dedicated in 1508 to St-Calais. The nave was destroyed during the XVII century. It was the private chapel of the royal couple. In the immediate vicinity of the castle, the vast collegiate church, St-Sauveur, was used for large ceremonies; it was destroyed after the Revolution.

The façade of the chapel, decorated with the initials of Louis XII and Queen Anne de Bretagne, was redone during the XIX century. The interior is entirely in Gothic style with pointed arch vaulting, keystones and tiles with heraldic decorations.

The Francis I wing, with its monumental staircase.

The Room of the Two Fireplaces, with Renaissance style furniture, in the Francis I wing.

Francis I wing. In the long series of constructions undertaken by Francis I, a prince "marvellously dedicated to buildings", Blois was the first in chronological order: the Francis I wing was commenced in 1515, that is at the beginning of his reign, and work was completed before 1524, marking the death of Queen Claude of France, whose initials and emblems are associated everywhere with those of the king. Built only 15 years after the Louis XII wing, the Francis I wing is very different. During these 15 years, French art changed

The first room on the first floor, with the monumental Francis I period fireplace.

radically in contact with Italian art. The Francis I wing is one of the very first masterpieces of the French Renaissance.

The overall appearance of the façade looking on to the courtyard is Gothic in style on account of the lack of symmetry and due to the traditional French animation of the upper parts of the building. The steep slate roof is embellished by large chimney stacks and imposing skylights and emphasized by an openwork balustrade. But the decorative system is completly new: the windows are framed by pilasters superposed from one level to another. Their interlacing, with horizontal mouldings separating the storeys, gives rise to chequerwork which was very much imitated, becoming the typical order of castles of the Loire. The remarkably wide cornices bear several rows of ornaments all borrowed from Italian architecture. The Italian influence can likewise be seen in the gables of the skylights with their old-fashioned niches and their puttos. As a concession to tradition, the emblem of the king, the salamander (whose motto means: "I encourage good and I stifle evil"), is sculptured eleven times in high relief on the Francis I façade.

The staircase, which was at the center of the façade before Gaston

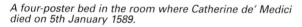

A four-poster bed in the room where Catherine de' Medici died on 5th January 1589.

d'Orléans began to modify the château, is a masterpiece. When the Italianate straight flights of stairs appeared in the Loire Valley after the Gothic period, the shape of the spiral staircase in a protruding octagonal cage was considered rather ordinary. The originality of the solution adopted here lies in the lattice-work of the walls between the corner buttresses. This staircase, with its three floors of balconies looking on to the Court of Honor, was perfectly suited to the pomp of the more and more sumptuous royal ceremonies.

Gaston d'Orléans wing. The building at the back of the courtyard was built between 1635 and 1638 for Gaston d'Orléans, Louis XIII's brother, exiled to Blois due to his perpetual intrigues against the king.

The severe style of this classic building does not harmonize with the fantasy and rich decor of the Renaissance constructions which would have disappeared if the project had been completed. The architect, François Mansart, had in mind a grand palace, with four wings around the courtyard and a complete rearrangement of the approaches with terraced gardens towards the Loire, as well as a fore-court surrounded by porticos, etc. This overly ambitious project was abandoned in 1638. Only the wing at the back was built and even this was never completed. Gaston d'Orléans passed the rest of his life in the Francis I wing, looking out on his unfinished masterpiece.

Nowdays the Gaston d'Orléans wing houses the Municipal library and two large halls used for concerts, conferences and exhibitions.

Francis I wing. On ascending the famous staircase to enter the Francis I wing, one notices the repetition of curved lines in the shape of the stairs, handrail, cornices and ribbed vault. The medallions of this vault bear the initials and emblems of Francis I, of his wife Claude of France (the "C" and the ermine), and of his mother Louise of Savoy (the swan pierced by an arrow, the crossed wings).

The first hall one enters on the first floor is formed by two halls joined together during restoration in the mid-XIX century. The Francis I apartments were largely restored during that period by the architect Duban: the tile flooring was redone and the walls and beams were repainted. The internal fittings were rebuilt with the exception of the chimney-pieces decorating the large hall and one of the door-frames. The elements which have been preserved are characteristic of early Renaissance sculpture: sumptuous detailed bas-relief decorations, sculpted

Door and Boiseries of the oratory giving access to Catherine de' Medici's workroom.

with motifs of foliated scrolls, shells, horns of plenty and emblems. Over a period of fifteen years, the Francis I wing was gradually renovated and furnished: Italian style tables, Flemish tapestries, chairs and, above all, chests which continued to be the basic piece of furniture during the Renaissance as in the Middle Ages.

The second hall, known as the Guardroom, features an extraordinarily large piece of embroidery dating back to the XVII century and portraying religious subjects. Two oft-reproduced portraits of the poet Ronsard, one painted and the other sculpted, can also be seen. In fact, tradition has it that it was at the castle of Blois during a ball that Ronsard met Cassandra Salviati to whom he dedicated

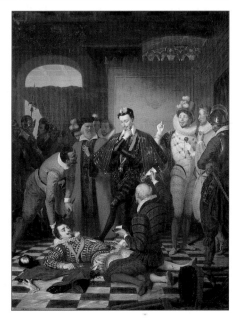

Charles Comte's portrait depicting the king and the Duke of Guise, at Blois, the day before the assassination (top), and the assassination of the Duke of Guise depicted in the painting by Durupt (right).

Marie de' Medici

The determined and self-willed Marie de' Medici (Florence 1573 – Cologne 1642) was the daughter of Francesco I, grand duke of Tuscany, and of Joanna of Austria. In 1600 she married Henry IV, king of France and Navarre, and gave him six children. After the assassination of her husband in 1610, Maria was named regent for her son, the future Louis XIII. Guided by her favorite, Concino Concini, she reversed Henry's anti-Spanish policies and supported the Catholic cause. This stance earned her the hostility of the court and later, following the murder of Concini (1617), exile to Blois, decreed by Louis XIII, who had in the meantime come of age to rule. Marie escaped from Blois and raised a revolt against her son. She was defeated, but in 1620, by intercession of Richelieu, obtained pardon from the king, who was nevertheless forced to send her into exile again ten years later, this time to Compiègne, after her unsuccessful attempt to have Richelieu dismissed. But Marie was not one to surrender unconditionally: she escaped again and from abroad continued to plot against her son, however ineffectually, until her death.

so many poems. A wooden panel dating back to the second half of the XVI century depicts a ball at the court of the Valois which could have taken place in Blois. It mainly represents the volta, an Italian dance introduced by Catherine de' Medici.

The old building's Medieval structure can clearly be seen on passing from that hall to the following gallery: the door recess in the 2 metres thick rampart and rounded sections of the tower to the right on entering. The gallery itself was also built by Francis I and opens outward mainly through sorts of loggias, variants of the loggias of Bramante at the Vatican, which in the past overlooked vast gardens. The royal busts assembled in this gallery are a reminder of the long visits paid by Catherine de' Medici and her children to the castle of Blois during the last third of the XVI century and of the interest paid by their successor, King Henry IV, to the castle of Blois where he had a 200 metres long gallery built along the edge of the gardens; unfortunately, however, it fell to ruin during the XVIII century.

At the back of the gallery one can admire a Spanish or Portuguese "Bargueño", in the numerous drawers of which precious collections were stowed away.

After the ante-room in an old tower dating back to the XIII century set against the rampart (note the thickness of the four walls of this room), one enters the royal bedroom occupied on several occasions by Catherine de' Medici, forced to flee from Paris which was shaken by religious troubles at the time. She died there on the 5th January 1589, a matter of days after the Duke of Guise was assassinated. This room, thus named Catherine de' Medici's bedroom, was decorated with the initials of Henry II and of the queen when it was restored during the XIX century.

During the XVI century, the room was not as private as one is made to believe nowadays. Guests were happily received there. The recess in the wall no doubt enhanced the importance of the chair set on a small platform and sheltered under a dais where the queen sat. Various pieces of furniture, bought or donated over a period of fifteen years, recreate the atmosphere of a bedroom. The portraits on the walls are a reminder of Catherine de' Medici's preference for the art of portaiture whose development she encouraged during the XVI century.

The nearby chapel features interesting painted woodwork and, in the apse, one can admire an attractive piece of sculpture. The study is the most interesting room in the Francis I wing because it has kept its original carved wainscoting: its 237 panels, which are all different, offer a complete repertory of the decorative motifs used at the beginning of the Renaissance: arabesques, horns of plenty, masks, dolphins, etc. This room is likewise famous on account of its secret wallcupboards known as "poison" cupboards after the novelist Alexandre Dumas. But it is not known, in fact, whether Catherine de' Medici, ever hid poison there!

While the second floor of the Francis I wing was being renovated it was the scene of a tragic event which occupies an important place in French history. On the 23rd of December 1588, Henry, Duke of Guise, was assassinated by order of King Henry III of France.

This assassination was the outcome of religious strife that ravaged France during the reigns of the children of Henry II and of Cather-

A view of the Hall of the Estates General.

ine de' Medici initiated by the fanaticism of the Protestants supported by Elizabeth of England and the intransigence of the Catholics, reunited in the bosom of the League, and encouraged by Philip II of Spain. The authority of the king was perpetually combatted by this League, and in particular by its head, the Duke of Guise. The situation worsened during the meeting of the Estates General of the kingdom at the castle of Blois in October 1588: Henry of Guise took over and openly ridiculed the king, who resolved to assassinate him. The pictures in the Cabinet room and in the king's bedroom illustrate this tragic event as well as the assassination of the Cardinal of Lorraine, brother of the Duke of Guise, which took place 24 hours later. On returning to the first floor, one reaches the hall of the Estates General. Let us remember that it was the great hall of the fortress of the Counts of Blois, built at the beginning of the XIII century. It was in this great hall – one of the oldest still extant in a Gothic castle – that the Count of Blois exercised his authority, dispensed justice and received the homage of his vassals. While it was part of the royal castle, it housed on two occasions, under Henry III in 1576 and 1588, the Estates General of the kingdom of France. The arrangement of this hall with its two naves separated by a row of columns recalls the chapter-house of an abbey. The capitals date it back to the beginning of the XIII century. The naves are not covered by stone vaults but by a panelled ceiling consisting of small planks of wood juxtaposed. The interior decoration was repainted during the XIX century.

A room of Louis XII's old apartments, now part of the Museum of Fine Arts.

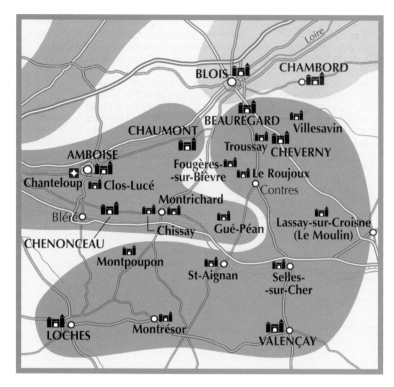

Cheverny, a Gobelin tapestry depicting the "Abduction of Helen of Troy" (XVII century).

55

BEAUREGARD

T he castle of Beauregard, between Bois and Cheverny is situated on the edge of the Russy forest and is enhanced by a large park of its own. Originally, Jean Doulcet, former Master of the Chamber of the Oboles to Charles of Orléans, lived there in 1495. René, bastard of Savoy, uncle to Francis I received this estate as a gift in 1529 from his royal nephew. In 1545 the poet Jean du Thier, protector of Ronsard and Du Bellay, secretary to King Henry II bought this hunting lodge for two thousand gold écus and transformed it into a castle. In 1617 the property was purchased by Paul Ardier, treasurer to three kings (Henry III, Henry IV and Louis XIII). Afterwards, it changed hands several times and was owned by the Fieubert family, the Marquis de Gaucourt; in 1816 it belonged to the Viscount de Préval, the Countess of Ste-Aldegonde, in 1850, the Count of Cholet, Louis Thillier, and then, in 1907 it became the property of the Gosselin family, grandparents of the current owners, M. and Mme du Cheyron du Pavillon.

The castle hosted many important guests. Francis I stayed at the hunting lodge. In 1626 Richelieu preferred Beauregard to Blois which was considered unsafe and ideal for plotters; and Anne-

Marie-Louise d'Orléans, duchess of Montpensier, known as "Mademoiselle" stayed there several times. Over the centuries the castle was modified considerably. The original residence was enlarged by Du Thier in 1545 with the hunting lodge, two parallel structures connected by two superposed galleries, flanked by two pavilions. In 1617 the old building was torn down. Ardier ordered the construction of two, lower symmetrical wings and began work on the Portrait Gallery.

In the XIX century the Marquis of Gaucourt destroyed the north wing, the chapel and the frescoes by Nicolò dell'Abate. English gardens were designed. The Countess of Ste-Aldegonde doubled the western gallery and added a neo-Gothic oratory which no longer exists. In 1850 the architect Jules de la Morandière restored the castle and especially the southern wing which was returned to its XVI century dimensions.

Starting in 1912 Thillier began new restorations, remodelling the roofs and unifying the east and west façades in the Renaissance style. Today, in its "reduced" size, the castle of Beauregard still has the charm of a XVI century residence. The current owners have also restored the XVII century spirit of the annexes. The interior is extremely interesting. First, there is a quite remarkable **Portrait Gallery**. It still has the original Delft tile floor (depicting infantry and cavalry troops on parade), boiserie and ceiling with paintings by Pierre Mosnier. The gallery contains 363 portraits from the first of the Valois to Louis XIII . The Cabinet des Grelots, or room of the bells, created in the XVI century is entirely covered by sculptured gilt decorations by Francisque Scibec de Carpi.

The extraordinary Portrait Gallery, with 12 panels containing a collection of portraits of the illustrious men from the courts of 12 kings of France, from Philip VI to Louis XIII.

CHEVERNY ⟐

W hat strikes one most about Cheverny at first glimpse are its majesty and symmetry. It consists of a tall building joined by two wings to square pavilions covered by rounded roofs surmounted by lanterns. Its Renaissance architecture has been clearly influenced by the Classical period; this can be seen from the series of niches with busts that lighten the façade.

The castle's outbuildings house an exceptional Trophy Room, containing a collection of over two thousand deer antlers, and a kennel housing a pack sixty strong trained for coursing. The owners of Cheverny regularly organize hunts, which are greatly appreciated by hunting circles.

Unlike other castles, such as Blois and Chambord, whose interiors are almost empty, Cheverny boasts magnificent, intact furnishings dating back to the Louis XIII epoch. In fact the castle

has always benefited from the rare privilege of belonging to the same family (except for a brief period in 1564 when Diane de Poitiers lived there), and this has enabled great unity of taste and style.

We know that in 1315 the castle of Cheverny was a simple press. At the time, the Hurault family was

already famous; from father to son, they were secretaries, ministers and chancellors under various sovereigns, from Louis XII to Henry IV. In 1490 Jacques Hurault, Louis XII's intendant, decided to transform the press into a castle; this gave rise to a building "with a moat, drawbridge, turrets, barbicans and other forms of defence". This castle, of which only a drawing remains, appears to have been built where the outbuildings stand at present. A document relates that the existing castle, built in 1634, was erected "on the site of the previous one", but it remains to be seen if the phrase "on the site" means "on the same site" or "in place of". In any case, Cheverny's history is connected to a famous, dismal event, as related in the "Memories" of the Marquis Durfort de Cheverny, a historian who lived in the castle during the Revolution. Henri Hurault inherited the estate in 1599 at the age of 24. At a very young age, he had married the eleven-year-old Françoise Chabot, but the couple had lived almost always apart because of the long military campaigns in which Henri participated. One day as a young man he was in Paris at King Henry IV's court; as a joke, he raised two fingers to look like horns above Henry's head. His gesture was met with laughter but a mirror revealed to the count that he himself was the laughing stock. Without saying a word, the young man mounted on horseback and rode until he arrived home at dawn.

In great silence, the count had the doors opened and arrived unexpectedly in his wife's bedroom; the story goes that the young page with whom the countess consoled herself over her husband's long absences jumped out a window just in time, breaking a leg. The count

The monumental fireplace adorning the royal bedroom.

The Guardroom, with its stupendous Renaissance fireplace.

The large hall, with a portrait of the Countess of Cheverny, by Mignard, hanging over the fireplace.

killed him with his sword. Then, accompanied by a priest, he returned to his wife's bedroom, holding a glass of poison in one hand and a sword in the other, and told her that he would return within an hour, leaving the anguished woman to make the terrible decision. When the time was up, the count returned; his wife drank the poison and died. This must have been more or less how the story went, even if the parish register of St-Martin de Blois certainly gives a truer picture. In fact, it is stated that "On Saturday 26th January... the Countess of Cheverny was poisoned because she committed adultery and rumour has it that when the surgeons, William and son, opened her, they discovered a five and a half month old child, the same day a gentleman from Burgundy called Chambelin, suspected of being her lover, was killed in the said castle of Cheverny." No matter what really happenend, it remains certain that Henri Hurault, having accomplished his terrible mission, returned to Paris the same evening in time for the "coucher du roi" ceremony. When the king heard about the sad events for which in fact he was mainly responsible, he became most irritated and exiled the count for three years to the Cheverny estate. Here Henri Hurault fell in love with the daughter of his Knight Commander and married her; it was his second wife, described as being thrifty, intelligent and with great taste, who directed the works, enlarging and embellishing the castle; for this purpose, she commissioned the architect Bohier and the artist Jean Mosnier.

A direct descendant of the Huraults, the Marquis of Vibraye then handed on the tradition to his grandchildren, the Viscount and Viscountess of Sigalas, who inherited the estates on his death and who still today keep Cheverny's past splendour intact.

A room with Louis XV furniture.

VILLESAVIN

The castle of Villesavin is located in the heart of a beautiful forest, far from all inhabited areas, between Chambord and Cheverny. The castle's origins date from 1527 when Jean le Breton, lord of Villesavin, Secretary of Finance to King Francis I, and imprisoned at Pavia with him, was assigned to oversee and pay for important work on the castle at Chambord. He had his own castle built by the Florentine workmen who had been engaged at the royal estate. Work proceeded quickly and was finished in 1537. Villesavin remained in the Le Breton family until 1611 when Jean Phelypeaux, Count of Buzançay bought the property that his family would retain until 1719. In that year the farmer general of revenues, Adine became the new owner. In 1817 Count Auguste de La Palu restored the castle and modernized it according to his tastes. Since 1937 the estate has belonged to the De Sparre family.

From the outside, the castle without its round towers must have been quite futuristic for its era. It is a magnificently symmetrical structure that rises around the grand staircase. The novelty and clarity of the architectural concept were inspired by Italian villas. A magnificent Carrara marble basin carved by Florentine artists decorates the main courtyard which is a perfect square reached by a bridge over the recently restored moats. The low walls with high roofing make Ville Savin unique: 9 meter high walls have 11 meter high roofs. The unusual white stone dovecot still has its spiral staircase and 1500 compartments.

In the chapel one can admire beautiful, early XVII century frescoes, which unfortunately are in quite poor condition. The outbuildings, in a charming courtyard with an ancient lime tree house and interesting collection of old carriages that includes a child's carriage.

TROUSSAY ⛫

T he castle of Troussay is located near the castle of Cherveny, in a very wooded area.

The castle originated in the XV century. In 1546, the first known owner of record was Robert Bugy comptroller of the salt stores at Blois and the king's equerry. His descendents lived in the castle until the XVIII century. In 1732 Troussay was purchased by the Pelluys family who, through the Bégons were related to Colbert. In 1828 the castle was inherited by the historian Louis de la Saussaye. With the help of the architect de la Morandière he undertook the restoration of Troussay which was in "great disrepair". These restorations which "scrupulously respected the manor's proportions and physiognomy" preserved everything that could be saved. Many items from ancient monuments around the region further embellish the castle where Prosper Merimée is known to have stayed.

Outside, on the entrance façade with towers on either side, there is a capital originally from the castle of Bury. The northern façade develops around a XIX century tower with a porcupine, symbol of Louis XII that was salvaged from the Hurault palace at Blois. The two long structures of the annexes in the entrance courtyard give the manor the air of a traditional Sologne country house.

The gardens behind the castle have decorative trees, two small garden pavilions (XVII and XVIII century) and a French kitchen-garden. The interior of the castle was considerably restored during the XIX century. Note the external additions: colored windows from the Sardini and Guise palaces at Blois (XVI century), the dancing cupids painted in grisaille by Jean Mosnier (XVII century) and the exceptional example of early Renaissance ornamental sculpture on the door of the Bury chapel. The annexes host a **Museum of the Crafts and Traditions of Sologne**, that illustrates the various aspects of rural life.

LE ROUJOUX 🏰
The "Enchanted Castle" of Fresnes

The castle of Roujoux is located in the town of Fresnes, between Fougères-sur-Bièvre and Contres.

In 1080 Marie Frangal, daughter of the lord of Fougères was the first mistress of Roujoux. Between 1315 and 1440 Roujoux was divided into five small feifs that belonged to the castle of Blois. In 1450 Guillaume Paris reunited these five fiefs and described the estate as consisting of "one tile-covered house, another house that serves as a barn and a courtyard between them", separated by filled moats over an area of 11 ares. In 1528 Jacques des Pas de Feuquières sold Roujoux to Jean de Villebresme, chamberlain to the king. In 1549 Pierre de Villebresme built the left wing of the existing castle. In 1618 René de Maille-Bene-hart, gentleman of the King's Chamber, and Master of the Hunt in the county of Maine, rebuilt Roujoux and maintained the Ville-bresme residence in one wing. In 1777 the building, which then belonged to Louis Richou de Rochefort, was in extremely poor condition, and it was spared total destruction by the Revolution. In 1818 the property was divided up: the castle had 9 owners in less than 70 years! In 1827 the chapel was eliminated. In 1830 Colonel Carrel entrusted the castle to Binet a former officer of the Royal Guards who tore down the port, drawbridge and one of the towers in the Garden. In 1889 Roujoux was purchased by Gabriel de la Morandière, son of the architect who worked on the restorations at Blois and Chaumont.

Inside, in the gallery one can see a lovely XVII century fireplace. The painted doors and wall decorations were done by Gabriel de la Morandière (XIX century). The rooms are enlivened by automatons that tell the stories of the "Thousand and One Nights", an evening with the harpsichord, and the history of the castle, complete with sound. A lovely wooded park, the river, meadows, and moats give the entire place a tranquil country charm which is enlivened by barnyard animals, an aviary, peacocks, etc. The castle is called "enchanted" because in addition to the inside entertainment and the animals, there are outdoor play facilities for children, as well as picnic areas.

FOUGÈRES-SUR-BIÈVRE ⛫

L ike the other châteaux of the Loire, Fougères is also situated on the area of a Medieval stronghold with external defenses.

During the Hundred Years' War the castle was the scene of military action and the Black Prince destroyed a great part of it and all the defensive structures. Later, in 1470, the new owner was Pierre de Refuge, who held the offices of counselor for Charles of Orléans and then treasurer to the royal court under Louis XI. Economically well off, Pierre was able to undertake the reconstruction of the area around the central keep which the ravages of time and man had left fairly intact. The defensive walls and the circular towers which still flank the central part were thus completed, although not by Pierre but by his successor, his son-in-law Jean de Villebresme.

As can be noted from the internal courtyard, the complex still bears signs of its Medieval origin, untouched by the Italian Renais-

sance influences of the early XVI century. The towers are illuminated internally only by small windows – in line with the parameters of military structures – and are covered by steep conical slate roofs. The masonry construction in irregular stones and mortar differs from the more elegant structures that became fashionable later in which blocks of ashlar fit together perfectly. The low heavy arches of the courtyard lend a feeling of strength and sobriety to the entire ensemble, quite unlike the refined elegance introduced into French architecture by King Francis I when he returned from Italy. The presence of orifices for throwing molten lead, strong walls and defensive moats demonstrate that the castle was still thought of as a stronghold and not yet as a pleasant residence that was pleasing to behold and hospitable inside. Not until the XVI century were new wide windows cut into the walls of the rooms which only had enormous fireplaces. Worthy of note in the nearby town is the small church which still preserves many Romanesque features despite more recent remodelling.

LASSAY-SUR-CROISNE ⛪
(Le Moulin)

The isolated setting of this castle is striking for its freshness and tranquility, in the midst of green lawns and beautiful trees.
The castle was built by Philippe du Moulin between 1480 and 1506. According to legend he saved the life of King Charles VIII at the battle of Fornoue during the Italian Wars. He was governor of

Langres as well as advisor and chamberlain to Charles VIII. He married Charlotte d'Arbouges, widow of Jean d'Harcourt. From 1506 to 1900 the castle remained in the hands of Philippe's heirs, until the death of Edmond Chenu de Thuet, and in 1901 it was purchased by M. de Marcheville. The castle was in terrible condition. Restorations were entrusted to Charles Genuys, Inspector General of the Government Monument Service and the architect Pierre Chauvallon who directed the works from 1902 to 1910 seeking in every way to respect the original structure.
The castle was not remodelled and conserves nearly all its architectural purity. Built on the

model of Medieval fortresses, one can see a strong Italian influence (ornamental sculpture, dormer windows).

The castle stands on a rectangular plot of land isolated by filled moats that are fed by the Croisne. The small entrance castle with its two high towers and narrow embrasures, encloses the drawbridge. The footgate, and the carriage gate still have their original studded doors (XVI century). The cylindrical tower at the left corner is the only one still standing; the others were razed to ground level. The four-storey house has a charming, projecting oratory. It is built of red and black brick in a losenge pattern; stone is only used on the corners and window frames. On the west and southern walls, the bricks form a pattern of vertical rectangles, a watermill wheel (west) and a symbolic pattern (south) that is found on ancient monuments. Inside, between the entrance tower and the left corner tower, in the XVI century building, one finds the Guardroom, an old kitchen with crossed ogival arches that rest on a polygonal pillar. In the elegantly furnished living quarters (period furniture, objects, tapestries) one can see an interesting French-style joist with the original painted decorations.

The recently built (XIX and XX century) stone and timber annexes are fascinating and were used for location shooting of some episodes of the French television serial "Thierry la Fronde" in the 'sixties. At the entrance to the village a charming little church houses a statue of Philippe du Moulin, above which one can admire a lovely sixteenth century fresco depicting St. Christopher, the church of Lassay and the castle.

Two views of the château of Lassay-sur-Croisne,
surrounded by large moats, complete in its architecture
modelled on Medieval fortresses.

VALENÇAY🏰

T he name of Valençay probably derives from Valens, a Gallo-
   Roman owner of the estate which lies on a cliff overlooking the
valley of the Nahon river. The original nucleus of buildings began
to take form in the III-IV centuries. A massive stone tower that was
built between the X and the XI centuries was the distant ancestor
of the château we now see. The first real feudal castle was built at
the beginning of the XIII century, perhaps by Gauthier, lord of
Valençay. Inherited by the Chalon-Tonnerre family, it was restructured and enlarged. The so-called Guardroom, an immense vaulted room, dates to this period. It is situated under the court of
honor, access to which is from the subterranean areas of the castle
through a corridor which probably connected the castle to the fortifications built to the north and west of the château. The other two
sides were defended by the cliff and had no need of man-made
defenses.
During the XV century the seigniory of Valençay passed to the rich
d'Etampes family, who demolished the old manor around 1540 and
commissioned a sumptuous new residence. It is not certain who the
architect called in by Jacques d'Etampes was. The names of both
Philibert de l'Orme and Jean de l'Espine have been suggested but
no documentary proof in favor of one or the other exists.
Inspired by the neighboring castle of Chambord, Jacques d'Etampes
had the fine entrance pavilion, a sort of unusual tower, built. As at
Chambord, the three superposed orders of pilasters have sculpted
capitals. With its crown of machicolations, emphasized by an elab-

orate frieze, this fine ensemble is one of the masterpieces of the Renaissance.

The corner towers and the main bodies of the building, highlighted by the fine Italian Gallery, also date to this period.

At the beginning of the XVII century Dominique d'Etampes continued the construction, adding the west wing of the palace – the one overlooking the park, and the one towards the east. The courtyard that opened on the valley was closed by an arcaded wall which connected the two wings of the building. The interiors were decorated by famous artists, including Jean Mosnier, who also worked in Cheverny and at the Palais du Luxembourg. The enthusiastic description of the château which Mademoiselle de Montpensier entrusted to her "Mémoires" after a sojourn at Valençay dates to 1653.

In the second half of the XVII century, trials, family altercations and complex problems of succession led to the decline of the d'Etampes family and the property passed into the hands of the Chaumont de la Millière family. It was then bought in 1766 by Charles Legendre de Villemorien, who undertook new works of remodelling. The east wing and the arcaded wall were demolished to open up the view over the city.

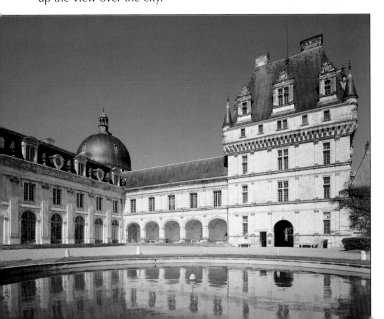

Around 1770 the west wing was also transformed with the construction of the elegant South Tower at the end towards the valley. De Villemorien also infused new life into the economy of the estate, creating a silk factory and a smithy and increasing commercial activity.

His son, Comte de Lucay, who escaped the guillotine during the Revolution, ceded everything to Talleyrand in 1802 since he was no longer able to bear the burden of the costs involved in maintaining the property. "Monsieur de Talleyrand, I want you to buy a fine estate, I want you to receive the members of the Diplomatic Corps, esteemed foreigners, I want people to want to come to your house and that being invited constitutes a reward for the ambassadors of the sovereigns who will content me..." With these words Napoleon Bonaparte had his minister of Foreign Affairs acquire Valençay, which was officially turned over in May of 1803 for the notable sum of 1,600,000 francs; Napoleon himself contributed to payment.

Chronicles relate that Talleyrand, accompanied by Catherine Worlée, took three days to visit the entire estate: the château with its more than 100 rooms, the park of 150 hectares, the woods, the lands, the fields, the vineyards, 99 farms... for a total of 19,000 hectares, one of the largest feudal estates in France. As Napoleon had desired, for more than a quarter of a century the most important personalities of the time vied with each other to be received at Valençay by the great diplomat.

Laying the blame for the undertaking of the war in Spain on Talleyrand, Napoleon, who intended to use Valençay as he pleased, sentenced that it was to become the dwelling place of the Princes of Spain and their following for the circa six years they were in exile. When they arrived in May of 1808 the château proved insufficiently large to house their numerous following, who had to be lodged in the city, provoking considerable confusion.

A corner of the hall.

The bedroom of the King of Spain Ferdinand VII,
exiled to Valençay from 1808 to 1814.

To alleviate the gilded imprisonment of the princes, Napoleon ordered the unwilling Talleyrand, host-jailer, to construct the theatre near the orangerie: a real theatre in all senses, large enough to hold 150 spectators, with a stage as deep as the entire hall. The rich decoration of the interior is attributed to the Adam brothers, famous Scotch architects. It was inaugurated in 1810 and the most famous actors of the time appeared there. Some of the stage sets which were made in Paris have remained at the theatre which will soon be in use once more.

It was also at the time of the sojourn of the Spanish princes that the park was completely surrounded by walls as a security measure. In 1806 Talleyrand had it turned into an English garden, setting up scenic routes and commissioning the architect Renard to build exotic constructions (the Turkish pavilion, the Cossack's house, the Egyptian temple, the Chinese bridge). The only building still extant is the one created for dances and other entertainment and which was later transformed into a hunting lodge. The imposing monumental staircase which joined the Duchess's garden to the vegetable garden has also disappeared. The park does, however, still contain the ice room which is as yet in working order.

On March 12, 1814, the Princes of Spain returned to their native land, and after the Congress of Vienna, the fall of the Empire and the return of the Bourbons Talleyrand retired to Valençay with

The bathroom, with furnishings and decorations dated 1830.

Dorothy, his nephew's wife and future Duchess of Dino, where he ordered considerable renovation to be carried out and cancelled all traces of the Spaniards. The château was reborn: sumptuous receptions and banquets marked by the culinary skill of the great Carême were given; the smithy, the saw mills, the silk factory were once more put into working order; sheep raising was augmented by crossbreeding with merinos from England.

Among the important persons who stayed in the château during the last years of Talleyrand's life were Duke Paul de Noailles, Princess de Lieven, Countess Tyskiewicz, Thiers, Balzac, Decazes, the Duke d'Orléans and, in 1834, George Sand.

Talleyrand died in Paris on May 17, 1838 and was buried in Valençay as he had asked. The château and the estate passed to Louis de Talleyrand-Périgord named Duke of Valençay by Charles X. Since 1980 the château has been the property of a Departmental Association which administers it.

Talleyrand's bedroom.

SELLES-SUR-CHER 🏰

The castle of Selles-sur-Cher is located in the town of the same name on the banks of the river Cher.

Originally, the castle was a fort built by Thibaut Le Tricheur over Merovingian foundations. In 1142 Ginon de Méhun built a stronghold that Richard the Lion-Heart captured, taking advantage of the absence of Raoul de Méhun, Ginon's son, who had left on a Crusade. Richard destroyed the Medieval complex. In 1212 Robert de Courtenay ordered the fortifications rebuilt. His nephew, Beaudoin, Emperor of Constantinople stayed there, the five towers still standing today date from that period (originally there had been seven).

The Black Prince took the castle in the XIII century. In 1370 Du Guesclin captured it. In 1604 Philippe de Béthune, Sully's brother built a new castle with great Parisian and royal influence. In 1787 the main building was destroyed, and then it was totally demolished by the Bande Noire in 1813. Charles VII stayed there several times, as did Louis XI and Louis XII, in 1471 and 1509, respectively. Maria Sobieska, Queen of Poland lived there in 1696. Outside, the access bridge is flanked by two, XVII century stone and brick structures in the style of Place des Vosges in Paris. These two buildings are connected by a long wall with arcades, that can be walked on. At the far end of the park with its centuries old trees (including one of the oldest cedars of Lebanon in Europe) stands the Gilded Pavilion. It is an elegant, structure, decorated in the Italian Renaissance style, that Philippe de Béthune added to his XIII century fortress. The complex is surrounded by water filled moats that are crossed by four bridges. In the building to the right (the Béthune Pavilion) there is a fine guards' room, and the bedroom of Maria Sobieska, with the raised, Baroque bed. During the summer the rooms in the Gilded Pavilion come alive with performances depicting castle life: cooking, meals, evening games, library, etc.

The château with its monumental staircase.

St-Aignan reflected in the Cher.

ST-AIGNAN-SUR-CHER 🏯

On the banks of the Cher, embraced by narrow Medieval streets overlooked by the church and château, St-Aignan is today a flourishing industrial town. But centuries ago, it was the object of a long dispute between the Counts of Blois and Anjou. For many years, the stone fortress built on a rise, inside the town-walls, overlooked the roads crossing the area until, during the Renaissance, the Dukes of St- Aignan made it their luxurious residence. Between the end of the XV and the beginning of the XVI centuries, a new château was built, in stone and brick, which has reached the present day intact except for the western pavilion which was refurbished in 1858 and 1890, and the terrace overlooking the wooded Cher valley.

MONTPOUPON

This château rises in an isolated position between the valleys of the Indre and of the Cher. It stands in a clearing at the conjunction of three small valleys which are traversed by five brooks. The road that connects Loches with Montrichard passes by the front of the building which has a particularly elegant aspect.

The castle was begun in the XII-XIII centuries, as indicated by the oldest extant parts. The cylindrical keep, which widens slightly at the base, dates to this period. This massive structure is typically Medieval in the limited number of narrow windows which appear only above a determined height, in the widening of the summit and the stone bracket supports, and in the presence of small windows and arrowslits on top.

A long wing for the apartments is set against the keep with its conical roof. The diversity of architectural concept identifies them as XV and XVI century additions. True symmetry is lacking in the façade of the château, which is marked by a play of dark and light in which the masonry of the walls contrasts with the lighter color of the corner stones and of the reinforcements at the windows. The left side terminates in a slender angle tower, with elongated windows with architraves, thus balancing the tower of the keep which rises behind it. The right side consists of a wing with lodgings characterized by faceted polygonal stonework. Dormers with triangular dec-

The postern of the château, dating to the XVI century.

orative superstructures are set into the high pitched slate roofs of the central block. The whole complex is surrounded by a low encircling wall which incorporates a cylindrical tower with a conical roof and a postern dating to the XVI century. Square in form, the latter has corner towers (the ones on the façade are set on jutting corbels) between which is the portal, a window, and a dormer. The gate leads to the court of honour with the castle well.

The building was originally used by gentlemen when they went hunting and for a long time it belonged to the De Prie family, which included Louise de Prie, governess of the French heirs to the throne. Today the manor belongs to the family of De la Motte St-Pierre.

MONTRÉSOR 🏰

The castle overlooks the village of Montrésor: it is located on an old road, flanked by recently restored houses. The castle offers a marvelous view of the picturesque village and the Indrois valley. At the beginning of the XI century Fulk Nerra, great builder and daring warrior, built a fortress on a rocky peak over the Indrois valley to block access to the plateau. In 1188 Philippe Auguste took possession of the castle and gave it to André de Chauvigny. In 1433 the castle served as prison for Georges de la Trémouille, a minister to King Charles VII. In 1493 the Basternay family turned it into a "salon" for the distinguished, and made the castle into a country home. Ymbert de Basternay was a confident and advisor to Louis XI, Charles VIII, Louis XII and Francis I. In 1849 Count Xavier Branicki, a Polish emigré, restored the castle. During the Crimean War he accompanied Napoleon III to Constantinople and tried to raise a Polish regiment.

The castle can be reached via a door that dates from the XII century, the same period as the corner towers. A wall, actually remains of the XI century fortress, surrounds the castle. Inside, in the middle stands the residential building that was erected in the XVI century with its mullioned windows, dormer windows and two towers with machicolations. The interior of the castle was restored and remodelled in the XIX century. The furnishings date from the era of the Count Branicki. There are mementoes of his military career, hunting trophies, and French and Polish paintings. There are some interesting bas-relief wood sculptures depicting the battles between Jean III Sobieski, King of Poland, and the Ottomans, early Italian paintings, and fine porcelains all worthy of the visitor's attention.

LOCHES

The history of the château of Loches is intimately tied to the history of France as far back as the X century. At that time a wooden tower for defense rose on the highest point of a rocky plateau. It was connected to the surrounding countryside by tunnels excavated in the rock. At the beginning of that century the feudal domain belonged to Fulk I the Red, Count of Anjou, whose descendant Fulk Nerra created one of the first square forts in stone here.

Fulk Nerra made a name for himself in French history as a warrior. He was already count at the age of 17 and spent all his life feuding with the neighboring Counts of Blois. Despite the fact that he was the son of Fulk the Good (a man of learning and of wit, famous for his phrase to Louis V "an ignorant king is nothing but an ass with a crown"), Nerra sullied himself with more than one sin and went on pilgrimage to Jerusalem three times to expiate.

Aside from this, the birth of military architecture in stone owes a great deal to Fulk Nerra. He was a great builder of defensive works and realized several dozen forts based on new dictates which at the time made them impregnable. The tower at Loches, with a base measuring 25 by 15 metres, was built between 1005 and 1070. Its walls, over 38 metres in height and between two and three metres thick, are still pierced by holes for the scaffolding that was erected when it was built as well as holes for the suspension of the battlement platforms, wooden structures which were suspended in the

void and from which projectiles were hurled at the attackers. The three floors inside had chimneys whose vents can be seen from the outside.

In 1040 Nerra died at Loches, where he was buried, and his successor Geoffroi Martel of Anjou succeeded in defeating the Counts of Blois at St-Martin-le-Beau.

The house of Anjou thus came into possession of Loches – where other defenses were built towards the south – and the surrounding territory, until the last of the Fulks married the daughter of the Duke of Normandy, King of England. Their son, Henry Plantagenet, also became King of England, in 1154. But it was not long before disagreements arose between him and Philippe Auguste, King of

A view of the singular entrance.

France, who took a large part of their dominions from the Plantagenets. When Henry II Plantagenet died, his son Richard the Lion-Heart went to the Holy Land for the Third Crusade. Upon his return he fell prisoner to emperor Henry VI of Austria and Philippe Auguste was able to obtain various territories including Loches from Richard's brother, John Lackland. Free once more, Richard the Lion-Heart recaptured Loches in 1195 after only three hours of fighting. He died barely four years later in Chinon. His legitimate heir, Arthur, was assassinated by John Lackland against whom Philippe Auguste of France moved once more, taking Loches in 1205 after a year-long siege.

The Crown of France, which has owned the castle since then, incremented the defenses adding the Vieux Logis to the north, with a tower and a sentinel's walk, in the XIII century. In June 1429, after the taking of Orléans, Joan of Arc arrived here to convince Charles VII to move on Reims and be crowned king. And it was this same Charles VII who in 1444 had Agnès Sorel, the lovely lady-in-waiting who became the first mistress of a king in the history of France, stay in one of the towers here. Known as the lady of Beauté (both for her beauty as well as for the estate of Beauté-en-Champagne given to her by the king), Agnès was only twenty when Charles, in his forties, fell in love with her. Agnès took an interest in the affairs of court and loved to surround herself with luxury, so that the king often gave her jewels and rare oriental products. Despite this she was very devout and was a benefactress of the local church of Notre-Dame in Loches, today known as St-Ours.

This church had been built on the land belonging to the fort between the XI and XII centuries. Palmettes, human figures, monsters and animals of obvious Romanesque origin decorate the portal, above which is an "Adoration of the Magi". At present the interior dates in part to the XI century and in part to the XIV and XV centuries.

Agnes died in 1450, at only 28 years of age, apparently due to complications arising from a difficult pregnancy. Even so rumors were that she had been poisoned by the dauphin who had tried to seduce her, forcing her to leave Chinon for Loches. Agnès requested that she be buried in the church she had endowed and to which she left an inheritance of 2,000 gold scudi. With the accession of Louis IX the monks asked to be allowed to transfer the mortal remains of the king's mistress from the church to the castle since a sinner could not be buried in a holy place, but the threat of having to return the gifts she had bestowed made the monks think twice and the tomb of the lady of Beauté, with its sculpture and its alabaster, remained in the church up to the French revolution.

During the XV century the Kings of France completed the Vieux Logis with new dwelling constructions, with the New Tower and the Martelet. The Logis Royaux thus was eventually comprised of a XIII century tower and a wall, a block of constructions with a XIV century guard tower, and a hunting pavilion dating to the XV century, contemporary with still another bastion in which passageways for various streets were opened (Porte des Cordeliers, tower of St. Anthony).

The new wing contains the chapel of Anne de Bretagne, wife first of Charles VIII and then of Louis XII. When she was only 23, Anne had already suffered the loss of her parents, her husband and four

The room where, in 1429, Joan of Arc met the future King Charles VII. This event inspired a painting (right) by Alexandre Millin du Perreux (1764-1843).

children. The queen was fond of retiring into a small room she had had prepared in Loches, where she could pray. Silver Breton ermines were sculptured on the walls on a blue ground, and an altar and a fireplace decorated the corners of the room.

History narrates that during the Revolution the insurgents penetrated the château of Loches and devastated the Logis Royaux and Anne's chapel, as well as the prisons and the church of Notre-Dame. Here, mistaking the rich tomb of Agnès Sorel for that of a saint, they vented their wrath and destroyed it. Later the remains of Agnès were transferred to the castle and her tomb is now in one of the rooms of the Logis Royaux. The sculptured tombstone there is a copy of the alabaster original. It shows the lady of Beauté with her hands joined, watched over by two small angels and with two lambs at her feet.

Part of the castle of Loches was used as a prison and many famous personages occupied the cells from the XV century on. In 1469 Cardinal de la Balue was imprisoned in the circular tower. He had conspired against King Louis XI, causing him to be taken prisoner by Charles the Bold. Still today it is remembered that the cardinal was enclosed in a cage which he himself, the height of irony, had invented and which was known as the "little girl" because it was so small (1.50x1.75 m). Suspended beams and pulleys permitted the cage to be suspended several meters above the ground at night to avoid the possibility of flight.

Philippe de Commynes, famous historian, was also imprisoned in Loches. He betrayed Louis XI, embracing the cause of the nobles who had opposed the king. Transferred to the prison in Paris, he was finally rehabilitated under Charles VIII. Ludovico Sforza, known as il Moro, Duke of Milan, was also detained in the Martelet. This refined scholar had been taken prisoner at the battle of Novara and after an initial period in Bourges he was confined to Loches.

A portrait of Agnès Sorel, Charles VII's favourite, by Jean Fouquet, and, below, a detail of her tomb in white marble.

Because of his rank Louis XII permitted him to have various comforts such as the company of a court jester and of teachers and the use of furniture and a fireplace. He himself decorated the walls and barrel vault of the cell with a helmet, snakes, stars and various mottos (including "He who is not content"). For eight years, up to 1508, il Moro remained closed in this room. It is said that as soon as he was freed, he died at the sight of the light and open air.

Other rooms were occupied by Antoine de Chabannes and Jacques Hurault, bishops of Puy and of Autun, who took part in the plot against Francis I related to the revolt of the high constable Bourbon. The two prelates carved an altar and a Via Crucis on the walls of their cell during their stay in prison.

Many old tales tell of the innumerable rooms and subterranean caves (from which the rock had originally been quarried) under the castle of Loches. One of these tells of a governor of Loches, Pontbrilliant, who attempted to visit all the rooms of the castle and forced some of the ancient doors which he found barred. Following various underground galleries which went deeper and deeper into the rock, the governor reached a last door beyond which he found a room where he saw a tall man seated with his head between his hands. When he came closer, he realized that it was a cadaver which the air of the closed room had mummified. The wind from outside reduced the body and a coffer which contained carefully folded garments into dust. Some say this tale is not a legend at all but really happened, for some of the bones of the cadaver were exhibited in the church of Notre-Dame.

The frescoed prison where Ludovico Sforza, called il Moro, was detained.

One of the rooms in the dungeons of the castle that can be visited is the so-called interrogation room, the ancient torture room. Created in the middle of the XV century by Charles VII, it still preserves the bar with rings which imprisoned the ankles of the prisoners when they were slowly torn to pieces until they confessed their crimes. Ironizing on the harshness of the treatment, an inscription in the circular tower says "Enter, gentlemen, to the king, our Lord".

The Romanesque church of St-Ours, with its richly decorated portal.

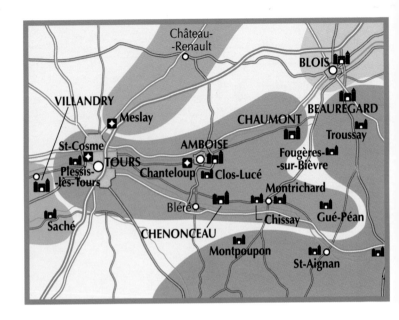

CHAUMONT

T he château of Chaumont (from "Chauve Mont" or Bald Hill, then changed into "Chaud Mont" or Hot Hill) stands on a hill next to the river Loire, in the midst of a dense wood of tall trees. As far back as the Middle Ages a castle already stood here. The first owner of Chaumont was Gelduin, who was saved from having to leave the castle to his daughter Claire when a son, Geoffroi, was born to him late in life. The boy's effeminate beauty earned him the nickname of "little girl" and despite his legendary physical resistance, Geoffroi never married and was for a long time considered a hermaphrodyte. The first castle in wood was destroyed, only to be reconstructed and then destroyed once more in 1465, when Louis XI used this as a means of punishing Pierre d'Amboise – the owner at the time – for having sided with the League of the Common Weal. Immediately after its demolition Pierre had work begun on the present castle, which was initially meant for military use and was not nearly as comfortable as it seems now. Italian Renaissance influences which lighten the austere west wing – the oldest – are evident. The windows were added later. The other wings are more recent and reveal a more generalized Renaissance character.

Catherine de' Medici

Daughter of Lorenzo II, duke of Urbino, and orphaned of both parents at an early age, Catherine (Florence 1519 – Blois 1589) was married in 1533 by her uncle, the Medici pope Clement VII, to the future king Henry II of France. Theirs was an unhappy union, tormented by the presence of the king's mistress Diane di Poitiers. Then, the turning point: at Henry's death in 1559, Catherine was appointed regent for three of her sons, who succeeded each other on the throne as Francis II, Charles IX, and Henry III, and showed her true Medici colors: she banished Diane from court, defended the crown through struggles with Catholics and Calvinists, Spain and the Guise brothers, and despite moments of crisis like the massacre of the Huguenots on 24 August 1572, succeeded in ferrying France, unharmed, from the Valois dynasty (extinguished with Henry III) to the Bourbon era.

Construction continued for three generations. Pierre was followed by his son Charles, the first of 17 brothers, and his grandson Charles II. The reliefs at the entrance refer to Charles II who succeeded in completing the château. Two entwined C's sculptured on the circular towers which flank the drawbridge refer to him and his wife Catherine. The French coat of arms with the initials of Louis XII and his wife Anne de Bretagne is set over the entrance door, while the towers bear the coats of arms of Charles II and his uncle Georges I, Cardinal of Amboise. Georges was an influential figure in the court of the king where he was ambassador and prime minister. While he barely failed to become pope after the death of Alexander VI Borgia, he did in any case guarantee a brilliant career under the crown to Charles II.

In 1560, after the death of Henry II, Catherine de' Medici bought the château. A beautiful room with tapestries is in fact attributed to her. In the brief period of her occupation another Florentine was also occasionally present in Chaumont, Cosimo Ruggieri, who had come to France together with the queen. Officially an astrologer based in the Breton Abbey of St-Mahé, he may really have been a charlatan or an occultist, although some say he was a true scholar. One of his laboratories and observatories, where Ruggieri often met with the queen, can be reached through one of the towers.

The bedroom of Catherine de' Medici.

The Amedée de Broglie stables (1877).

Some tales tell of how when the moon was full Ruggieri could see the king and his children in a magic mirror, revealing how many years they would live and how many years they would reign according to the number of revolutions the image made on the surface of the enchanted object. In any case Ruggieri was involved in various intrigues, both political and behind-the-scenes, prejudicial to the queen herself in whose palaces he had numerous observers. One of these conspiracies led to his detention in jail while his complices ended up on the gallows. His temporary rehabilitation did not hinder him from returning to prison accused of witchcraft against Henry IV.

The château of Chaumont was also offered by Catherine to the lovely Diane de Poitiers, formerly Henry II's mistress, in exchange for the larger building of Chenonceau. Actually Diane did live for a short while at Chaumont: her room – which can still be seen – and the sculptured coats of arms, identifiable by a horn, a bow and a quiver with her initials, date to this period.

Thereafter the castle passed to the Viscount of Turenne d'Auvergne, the Duc de St-Aignan Charles de Beauvillier, and to Jacques le Ray. Under Le Ray, during the XVIII century, the Italian Nini created a factory of fine ceramics (some of the medallions are now on exhibit in the castle) in the nearby annexes. Using the clay from the Loire, Nini produced many portraits of notables which became very popular and made Le Ray a rich man. During the Empire the famous Madame de Staël, whom Napoleon had enjoined to live at least 40 leagues from Paris, moved to the château where she surrounded herself with sympathizers.

In the XIX century the north wing was totally demolished so as to provide a panorama of the Loire and the surrounding park. The Broglie family also had the stables with the unique conical angular construction built. In 1938 the State bought the castle. Restored and furnished, it has since then been open to the public.

MONTRICHARD ⛫

The town of Montrichard, with its unmistakeable white houses, faces the river Cher, overlooked by the powerful bulk of the château. The original nucleus was a square stone bastion, built in 1120 by Hugo I d'Amboise, resembling the one in Loches. In the following centuries, starting with the restoration interventions requested by Richard Lion-Heart, fortified walls, cylindrical towers, a drawbridge and, finally, the rooms of the main residence were added, making Montrichard a proper, elegant château.

GUÉ-PÉAN ⛫

A few kilometers from Pontlevoy, in Loir-et-Cher, stands the château of Gué-Péan. Used as a hunting lodge, the complex dates to the XIV and XV centuries.
The ground plan is square and it now has a gateway at the center of the encircling walls. Two low semi-cylindrical towers, with terraces on top, flank the entrance. Three blocks of buildings arranged in a U pattern face onto the immense court of honour. The principal block, at the back of the courtyard, is flanked by cylindrical towers with conical roofs. The rather low facade has numerous win-

dows which mitigate the severe aspect of the castle and admit light. Elegant dormers with superstructures decorate the roof. The block on the left, which also has dormers, is in communication with a cylindrical tower that reinforces the front corner of the walls. The tower widens near the top, with sustaining brackets, and has a helmet-shaped dome with a small lantern, rather like the towers of the châteaux of Serrant and Valençay. The right wing, with a broad terrace, also communicates with a corner tower.

This one, quite unlike the other, is a simple cylinder with a conical roof.

Throughout the centuries numerous kings (Francis I, Henry II, Henry III) and famous men (La Fayette, Balzac) stayed in the elegant Renaissance apartments. Today the rooms of the château, which is owned by the Marquis of Keguelin, are open to the public. Of particular interest are the guardroom, the chapel, the hall and the library. The rooms are furnished with fireplaces, objects of art and antique furniture in Louis XV and Louis XVI style, with tapestries and paintings (including works by A. del Sarto, J.L. David, H. Rigaud, G. Reni, J.H. Fragonard), while the library contains a valuable collection of historical documents.

The hall, furnished in Louis XV style, with the monumental fireplace by Germain Pilon.

CHANTELOUP ▪

The highly original pagoda of Chanteloup, not far from Amboise, is all that remains of the château of Chanteloup, the "little Versailles" built by the Duke of Choiseul, a minister of Louis XV, where he was forced to live by the king after his fall from grace and subsequent removal from court in December 1770. In 1775, the duke directed his architect, Le Camus, to build the striking pagoda in homage to the loyalty of his friends. 44 metres high, this singular obelisk combines XVIII century French style with the typical features of Chinese monuments, in a completely unique union. Restored in 1910 by the architect René-Edouard André, today it hosts a permanent exhibition illustrating the historical events of the great château of Chanteloup, destroyed in 1823, and its charming gardens.

CHISSAY ⏶

Not far from Montrichard, in the valley of the river Cher, the château of Chissay-en-Touraine can be found, which was built in several stages between the XIII and XV centuries, even though the oldest tower dates back to the XI century and the last ones were added between the XVI and XVII centuries. In the XV century, the château was owned by Berard, treasurer to Charles VII. It then belonged to various wealthy families. Surrounded by a vast and luxuriant park, the château to this day still emerges from the vegetation in all its magnificence, with its cylindrical towers, characteristic dormers and numerous windows illuminating the interior of the château.

CHENONCEAU

I n 1243 the territory on which the château of Chenonceau is built belonged to the house of Marques, originally from Auvergne. A defensive fortress surrounded by moats and joined to the banks of the river Cher with a swing bridge and a mill stood on the site of the elegant Renaissance building now to be seen.

During Charles VI's reign the owner of the fort, Jean Marques, granted asylum to an English garrison. As a result the king had the defenses dismantled but salvaged the building and left the lands to the Marques. The family was always in debt and was forced to sell almost all its lands as time went on to Thomas Bohier, Intendent of Finance for Normandy. In the end he also bought the small fortress in 1512, but as it did not correspond to the latest Renaissance mode, Bohier decided to construct a new castle and tore down the one that was already there. The only remaining Medieval part is the tower of the keep, set in front of the castle which was mostly rebuilt.

A rectangular building with corner towers, erected around an internal vestibule with ogee vaulting, was built on what remained of the mill. There were four rooms on the ground floor, while a straight staircase (the spiral staircase was generally abandoned in the early XVI century) led to the first floor where there were four more rooms. The high costs of the construction seem to explain the motto the Bohiers had sculpted together with their initials T.B.K. "S'il vient a point, me souviendra" (If the castle is finished, it will preserve my memory).

Building activity, which Catherine Bohier, Thomas's wife, had overseen in the absence of her husband, was finished in 1521, when cardinal Bohier, archbishop of Bourges, consecrated the château

View of the château stretching along the river Cher, with the beautiful Catherine de' Medici gardens.

chapel. In 1524 Thomas Bohier died in Italy in the service of the king, and only two years later his wife also died.

Inherited by their son Antoine, the castle was soon confiscated by Francis I in repayment of various deficits for which Thomas was held responsible. Some say it was expropriated in 1533 because the king wanted to come into possession of this splendid building set in the midst of an estate abounding in game. And Francis I did go to Chenonceau, sometimes accompanied by a small group of close friends: the Queen Eleanor, his son Henry, Catherine de' Medici, his mistress Anne de Pisseleu lady of Heuilly and Diane de St-Vallier de Poitiers, his son's mistress. The castle was the scene of hunts on horseback, fêtes, suppers and intellectual activities, in accordance with the ideals of the period. Many stories, which were frequently slanderous, circulated regarding Diane de Poitiers. Some said that she had conceded her favors to Henry II's father, Francis I, so that he would intercede in favor of her father; others said that Francis I had asked her to put some sense into the head of his son Henry who was still very immature, and that she had answered that she would make him her lover. Whatever the truth, Diane had great influence over Henry II and once on the throne, in 1547, even though he was married to Catherine de' Medici, he continued to shower her with gifts. Even though he was 19 years younger than Diane, the new King of France used the crescent moon (symbol of the goddess Diana) as his emblem and dressed in the colors his mistress preferred, black and white. It was not long before the château of Chenonceau was also donated to Diane de Poitiers, despite the numerous legal cavils which decreed the building to be the property of the Crown and therefore inalienable. Together with the jewels of the Crown, Henry II assigned part of the royal fiscal revenue to his mistress. With this conspicuous sum at her disposal,

The sturdy arches rise over the waters.

Diane de Poitiers began the works of beautification including the layout of the garden with flowers, fruits and vegetables which at the time were considered exotic, such as melons and artichokes. She also had soundings taken of the bottom of the Cher for the construction of a masonry bridge, designed by Philibert Delorme and soon built.

Despite the passing of time Diane's beauty remained unchanged, as witnessed by the painting which shows her nude next to a stag. It is said that her secret was in diving into cold water as soon as she got up, riding and walking and then going back to bed until noon. However, in 1559, as Nostradamus had predicted, Henry II died after having been seriously wounded in one eye by a spear during a tournament. The queen, Catherine de' Medici, free to act as she pleased, began to vendicate herself of the lovely Diane and asked her to return the Crown jewels and the castle. After attempts at resistence, Diane was forced to give in and withdrew to the château of Anet where she stayed until she died at 66 years of age. Once she had Chenonceau, Catherine organized a great celebration in honor of her son Francis II and his wife, Mary Stuart. For these celebrations Primaticcio prepared a grandiose ornamental apparatus consisting of columns, statues, fountains, triumphal arches and obelisks, while a battery of 30 cannons was set up to fire salutes from the courtyard. New gardens, together with the annexes, were finished in 1568 and inaugurated with a great fête together with the ratification of the peace of Amboise.

Another unforgettable celebration was held in 1577 when Henry II returned from Poland for the succession of Charles IX. For the occasion the novel device invented by Henry for his festivities at Plessis-lès-Tours was used: the women disguised themselves as men and vice versa. Henry himself wore a gown of pink and silver brocade, with violets and diamonds in his hair and pearls at his neck. The depth of his decollete made Pierre de l'Estoile say that "it was difficult to tell at a glance if it was a king-woman or a queen-man".

In 1580 the architect Androuet du Cerceau began work on a new

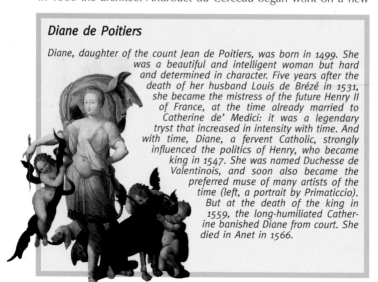

Diane de Poitiers

Diane, daughter of the count Jean de Poitiers, was born in 1499. She was a beautiful and intelligent woman but hard and determined in character. Five years after the death of her husband Louis de Brézé in 1531, she became the mistress of the future Henry II of France, at the time already married to Catherine de' Medici: it was a legendary tryst that increased in intensity with time. And with time, Diane, a fervent Catholic, strongly influenced the politics of Henry, who became king in 1547. She was named Duchesse de Valentinois, and soon also became the preferred muse of many artists of the time (left, a portrait by Primaticcio). But at the death of the king in 1559, the long-humiliated Catherine banished Diane from court. She died in Anet in 1566.

The bedroom of Catherine de' Medici.

wing that stretched out over the bridge on the Cher. The new building had two floors and its long facades were ably enlivened with windows, projections and dormer windows. The upper floor was to be used as a ball room and was decorated like the rest of the château with rich furnishings. The sumptuous festivals inspired by antiquity and myths, in which the ladies of the court often appeared half naked (hoping to gather useful reserved information to pass on to Catherine), ended when in 1589 the queen mother died in Blois. Her testament entrusted the château of Chenonceau to Louise de Vaudémont, wife of her son Henry III. A few months later – in August of 1589 – Henry was killed by Jacques Clément. It is said that before he drew his last breath the king dictated a letter to his wife in which he said: "My beloved, I hope to be well: pray God for me and do not move from there". These words may have induced the queen to stay in the palace until she died. All bright furnishings were done away with and were replaced by black drapes and attributes of death. In response to her desire for prayer the Ursuline nuns

H. Rigaud (1659-1743), portrait of Louis XIV.

came to live in the palace. She dressed in white – the color of royal mourning according to an ancient tradition – ever after until 1601 when the "White Dame" died. The château was inherited by Françoise de Mercoeur, wife of César, Duke of Vendôme. From then on the Kings of France stopped there only rarely. The last French sovereign to stay in Chenonceau was Louis XIV in 1650.

The state of neglect the Vendômes and the Bourbon-Condés had left the building in was briefly interrupted when one wing was used as a Capucine monastery. A drawbridge meant to isolate the monks from the rest of the world remains from this period.

In 1733 the Duke of Bourbon sold the castle to Claude Dupin, a wealthy financier. His wife, a lover of art, the sciences, letters and theater, created a bourgeois salon at Chenonceau which included the most famous names of the time. Fontenelle, Buffon, Montesquieu, Mably, Marivaux, Voltaire, Condillac, Madame de Tency and Madame du Deffand often stayed in the castle. Jean Jacques Rousseau became Madame Dupin's secretary and tutor for her daughter. He wrote: "One passed the time well in that lovely place and one ate well: I became as fat as a friar. We made music and recited plays. I composed an opera in verse entitled 'l'Allée de Sylvie' after the name of a boulevard in the park which skirts the Cher". In fact Madame Dupin had set up a small theater for the presentation of plays as well as a laboratory for the study of physics. The rooms of the preexisting apartments had also been rebuilt and made more comfortable.

In 1782 the château came to be lived in year round by its learned owner, who was so respected and loved by the local population that Chenonceau came through the Revolution unharmed. Abbot Lecomte, the local curate, intervened against the most ardent revolutionaries, telling them: "There is only one bridge between Montrichard and Bléré, and you want to tear it down! You are the enemies of the common good!" Madame Dupin was thus able to live in her castle until 1799 when she died at the age of 93 and was buried in the park.

XVI century Flemish tapestry depicting scenes of life in the château.

Abandoned, the château was sold in 1864 by the heirs to Madame Pelouze, who started to restore the castle to what it had been before Catherine de' Medici's transformations. Although some of the windows were eliminated, together with the caryatids on the facade, the monumental wing on the Cher was left untouched. The Pelouzes soon fell into ruin and in 1888 the château was confiscated by the Land Trust which sold it to Henri Menier, one of the wealthiest industrialists of the time. His brother and then his heirs are still the owners of Chenonceau.

One of the most meritorious acts in the history of the castle was when Gaston Menier, senator of Seine-et-Marne, transformed the building in 1914 into a temporary hospital where more than two thousand wounded were recovered up to the end of World War I. After having played an important role in the crossing of the partisan forces in the last war, the château with its bridge over the Cher has been completely restored and can be visited.

The entrance to the estate leads through a long avenue lined with age-old trees to a vast open space on the left of which are the gardens laid out by Diane de Poitiers. In the corner of the court of honour, surrounded by the waters of the river, is the cylindrical tower which, partly rebuilt, dates back to Medieval times. A drawbridge communicates with the ground floor of the castle where XVI century tapestries are exhibited in the guardroom. Sculpture in Carrara marble, including a "Virgin and Child", are to be found in the chapel. In addition to the green room and Diane de Poitiers' room, one can visit the gallery with paintings by Rubens, Primaticcio, Van Loo, Mignard and Nattier. A straight staircase leads to the first floor with the room of Gabrielle d'Estrées, the royal chamber (or of the Five Queens), Catherine de' Medici's room and that of Charles de Vendôme. The original cooking area and a unique, ingenious spit are still to be found in the kitchen.

In the annex, outside the château, is a small **Wax Museum**. The scenes reproduced include the most famous inhabitants of Chenonceau and the most outstanding episodes in its history. Catherine Bohier is shown with a minstrel, Diane de Poitiers is in the woods during a hunt and with Henry II, Madame Dupin is shown receiving Rousseau and Voltaire and, in an other episode, posing for the painter Nattier. There is also a reconstruction of the military hospital set up in 1914.

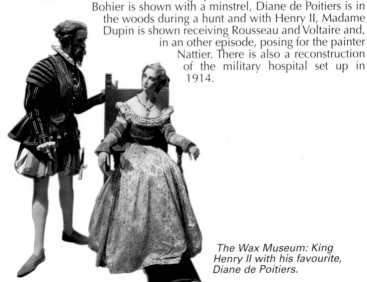

The Wax Museum: King Henry II with his favourite, Diane de Poitiers.

CLOS-LUCÉ 🏰

In 1214 Sulpice III, of the house of Amboise, gave the religious community of Moncé the land on which the château of Clos-Lucé was to be built. The edifice in pink brick and white stone rose at the time of Louis XI on the foundations of a precedent construction dating to the Gallo-Roman period. It was then bought by Etienne le Loup, an enterprising scullion in the kitchens of the royal castle of Plessis-lès-Tours, who in a lightning career had become one of Louis XI's favorite counselors. At the time, despite the gardens, the large dovecote in brick (still to be seen) and its vineyards, the château of Clos-Lucé was a fortified dwelling with its lookout tower, which is still in perfect condition, narrow windows, a postern and a drawbridge, traces of which are still visible next to the entrance.

When Etienne le Loup fell into disgrace, the château was bought on the 2nd of July, 1490, for 3,500 gold scudi by Charles VIII and improved, since it was now a royal residence, by skilled artisans, stone cutters and painters called in from Naples. The Chapel built in tuff for Queen Anne de Bretagne dates to this period.

A host of famous figures lived in the castle at one time or another: the young Duke of Angoulême, the future Francis I, his sister Margaret of Navarre, who probably began to write her collection of short stories ("Heptameron") here, Louise of Savoy when she was regent, Leonardo da Vinci, as well as other notorious figures of the time including the favorite Babou de la Bourdaisière, the captain of Henry III's guards Michel du Gast, who participated in the assassination of the Duke of Guise, St. Francis of Paola and Henry III.

The château then passed into the hands of the d'Amboise family who kept it from being destroyed in the period of the French Rev-

The hall where Leonardo da Vinci was received, with XV century furniture.

olution. It has now belonged to the St-Bris family for several generations.

In 1955 Hubert St-Bris decided to restore the castle to what it looked like when Leonardo da Vinci, the most famous of its many guests, lived there.

The complex restoration was entrusted to the architect of the Monuments Historiques, Bernard Vitry, and the work to specialized craftsmen of the Beaux-Arts. Thanks to them Leonardo's kitchen (the Old Guardroom), the Council Room and the subterranean chambers where Leonardo's splendid machines can be seen, the rooms of Margaret of Navarre and of Leonardo, each day come closer to their original appearance.

In the autumn of 1516, on invitation by Francis I, Leonardo left Italy, accompanied by a servant and his pupil Francesco Melzi. He reached France after a long trip on muleback, bringing with him "La Gioconda", "St. John the Baptist" and "St. Anne". In exchange for the château of Clos-Lucé (which was practically next to the palace at Amboise and at the time was called Cloux) and an annuity of 700 gold scudi, the king asked nothing of Leonardo but the pleasure of his conversation. The artist however amply paid back the king by organizing memorable fêtes and fantastic spectacles, such as the one of June 17, 1518, at which Galeazzo Visconti was present and of which he left a detailed description.

The admiration and love of the court did not however distract Leonardo from his studies and drawings, which he loved more than anything else. Despite the infirmity which is said to have involved his right hand, he obstinately dedicated himself to geometry, architecture, city planning and water works.

A large number of manuscripts produced after October of 1517 testify to the fervid activity of this period. These include a sheet of the

Codex Atlanticus with the annotation "Palazzo di Cloux d'Amboise, il 24 giugno 1518".

Probably from this period are the projects for the castle of Romorantin, those for the draining of the Sologne and those for houses which could be taken apart and which were designed specifically for the court, which was always moving from one place to another.

Many drawings preserved in the Royal Library of Windsor Castle (heads of old men, sketches for fêtes and carousels and drawings of the château of Amboise seen from one of the windows of Clos-Lucé) undoubtedly date to this period.

In his will of April 23, 1519, written by the court notary, Leonardo left all his books, his drawings and the instruments relative to the art of painting to Francesco Melzi; to his servant Battista and to Salay he left, in equal parts, the land he owned in Milan; to Mathurine, the maid, a dress of black wool lined with fur, a length of wool and ducats.

He died in the château on May 2, 1519, at the age of 67, and was buried in Amboise, in the royal cloister of St-Florentin.

When the cloister was destroyed, his mortal remains were transferred to the Chapel of St-Hubert in the château of Amboise.

Leonardo da Vinci

On 15 April 1452, the notary Ser Piero of Vinci, a small town not far from Florence, witnessed the birth of an illegitimate son to whom he gave the name Leonardo, who soon demonstrated a clear and lively intelligence and a remarkable capacity for learning. Thus, at just seventeen, Leonardo was sent to Florence, where he enrolled in the Compagnia dei Pittori and was apprenticed to Andrea del Verrocchio. In 1482 he moved to Milan, to the court of Ludovico Sforza ("il Moro"), where his genius as a painter, sculptor, and designer of court festivals unfolded and his unusual abilities in the fields of architecture, military engineering, and design of war machines also became well known. For many years after the fall of Ludovico, Leonardo traveled Italy from Venice to Mantua, from Florence to Urbino, from Cesena to Rome. Although admired and even contended by Isabella d'Este and Cesare Borgia, he was not always understood or appreciated in the world of artists and patrons. Louis XIII of France fol-

lowed his career attentively, commissioned many works, and provided incentives for his creativity. This profound relationship based on esteem and understanding created a lasting tie between the "volcanic" Leonardo, already famous for his inventions and extraordinary projects, and France. That France where the genius of Vinci settled finally in 1517, when he accepted the invitation of the young king Francis I to enter his service. To the Château de Clos-Lucé he brought a priceless collection of paintings, manuscripts, and documents, and worked for the king until his death on 2 May 1519.

Among Leonardo's machines note in particular the swing bridge, a futuristic assault tank, the catapult, with the machine-gun in the background, and the helicopter.

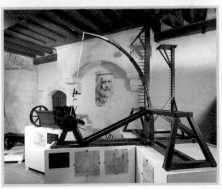

AMBOISE:

This picturesque town, in its delightful setting on the banks of the Loire is distinguished by its majesty and the live feeling of history. Residence of French Kings between the XV and XVI century, it was the birthplace of Charles VIII who also died there at the young age of 28 (in 1498); it was also home to Leonardo da Vinci during the last three years of his life which ended in 1519. Other highlights at Amboise include the **Clos-Lucé**; the **Church of St-Denis** (XII century with additions and changes made in the XV-XVI centuries); the **Hotel de Ville** (XVI century); and the **Church of St-Florentin** (XV century).

Amboise extends along the Loire, overlooked by the château, with its towers, churches and walls.

The Château of Amboise

Amboise first appeared in history around 503 when Clovis I, King of the Franks, and Alaric II, King of the Visigoths, met on the Ile St-Jean, in the center of the Loire, below the present castle.

Devastated by the Normans more than once, Amboise was first part of the possessions of the Counts of Anjou and then belonged to the famous house of Amboise-Chaumont until 1422, when it was inherited by Louis, Viscount of Thouars. Found guilty of plotting against the king, the owner of the château of Amboise was deprived of his lands.

From 1431 on, the castle belonged to the Crown. The "chastel d'Amboise" was no longer solely a fortress, but a royal residence and the city was benefited by the concession of receiving payment of the franchise. One of the great events in the reign of King Louis XI was the creation at Amboise of the Order of St- Michael on the first of August in 1469. That day the king gathered together fifteen of his most powerful barons in the chapel of St-Michael to acquaint them with the statute of this order of knighthood, whose foundation was of specifically political significance. The order of St-Michael represented the bond that tied the great lords and landed propri-eters to the royal Crown.

That day Amboise was the scene of a grand ceremony which remained in the annals of the kingdom.

The Queen Charlotte, who died there in 1483, was always surrounded by a large court as befitted her rank. She had almost 150 persons in her following and service. The apartments had been decorated and furnished in an effort to make her abode as pleasing as possible.

The serene life he had lived there when he was young explains why the new King Charles VIII was so attached to the château where he had been born and raised. It was in the Place du Carroir at Amboise that the young 13-year old dauphin received Margaret of Austria, granddaughter of Charles the Bold, whom his father had decided to give him as wife. Margaret was only three years old when she was engaged to Charles VIII and lived in the château of Amboise until 1492 when she had to return to Flanders with a heavy heart, ceding her post to Anne de Bretagne whom Charles VIII had married on December 6, 1491. Great construction works were undertaken at this time, financed by the income from the taxes. The plans were magnificent: "he wants to turn the castle into a city" exclaimed the Florentine ambassador when he saw the projects late in 1493. The area of the building had to be considerably enlarged. A large trapezoid divided into three courtyards took the place of the old Medieval fortress.

The two spiral turrets, the Minimes tower and the Hurtault tower, were important architectural innovations. As for the decoration, it was initially of French inspiration but later profited from the collaboration of Flemish artists and, after the return of the Italian expedition of 1495, of Italian artists. The furnishings were luxurious: Flemish and French tapestries, Damask curtains and Turkish carpets.

The hall of the States.

A view of the Louis Philip hall.

The imposing construction works which aimed at transforming the antique "oppidum" and the old fortress of the Counts of Anjou into an abode worthy of the Crown of France were interrupted by a mortal accident that befell the king in Amboise on April 7, 1498. While Charles was accompanying the queen in the Haquelebac gallery on his way to a ball game, it is said, he hit his forehead on a low door and died a few hours later. His successor was the Duke of Orléans who took the name of Louis XII, but the château of his choice was Blois, where much work was done during his reign and where he went to live with Anne de Bretagne, widow of Charles VIII, whom he married on January 8, 1499.

In 1500-1501 work was resumed and great quantities of stone were brought in to complete the buildings, particularly the Hurtault tower, and to create the gardens on the terraces above the Loire. With the accession of Francis I the château once more shone. From 1515 to 1518 the king sojourned in what he called "that sumptuous château" when he came to the banks of the Loire, and after Marignano he returned to Amboise in 1516. Queen Claude gave birth to her three children here.

During the reign of Henry II, Catherine de' Medici, who loved Amboise, lived there with the children of the royal house. The château was later abandoned by the court of Valois and if the young King Francis II and his wife Mary Stuart, the queen mother, children, servants and following all arrived there on February 22, 1560 at the beginning of the new regime, this was because they had to flee from Blois and the conspiracy plotted by Condé which broke out at the beginning of the month.

The famous conspiracy of Amboise was severely repressed and three years later, on May 19, 1563, the queen mother, Catherine de' Medici, and the Prince de Condé stipulated the treaty which put an end to the first religious uprisings and allowed freedom of worship to the Protestant aristocracy.

After these extraordinary events, the château of Amboise ceased to be a royal residence even though Louis XIII lived there off and on.

In 1627 it became part of the property of Gaston d'Orléans and in 1660 returned to the Crown of France. But at that time the château was no longer really liveable for it had in part been demolished. In 1762 the Duke of Choiseul bought the château, the baronage and the territory of Amboise which his heirs sold in 1786 to the Duke of Penthièvre. In the years which preceded the Revolution he ordered work, including new construction, to be done in the building, which was at the center of the duchy from 1787 on. During the Revolution the château was confiscated and once more despoiled. Army barracks were installed and a button factory was set up between the logis des Sept-Vertus and the chapel of St-Hubert.

But it was only later, under the First Empire, that Amboise was most seriously mutilated and even systematically demolished by the member of parliament Roger-Ducos, who as senator was a beneficiary of the settlement of Orléans and was assigned the château of Amboise as his residence. Lacking the means to maintain it, the only solution he found was that of largely destroying it. In 1815 it was restored to the heiress, the Duchess of Orléans.

When the Duchess of Orléans died in 1821, her son, the future King Louis Philip, inherited the château and the property of Amboise. Louis Philip acquired 46 houses and barracks which surrounded the château in rue des Minimes and at Porte Hurtault and had them torn down, freeing the towers and the encircling walls.

From 1848 to 1852 the château of Amboise had an unexpected guest, the Arabian emir Abd-el-Kader, who spent four years here until Napoleon III, prince and president, personally came to Amboise on October 16, 1852 to communicate his newly acquired liberty.

In 1974, when it was created, the St-Louis Foundation took over the administration of the château and now continues to carry out the restoration which was begun at the end of the last war.

The chapel of St-Hubert,
refined by the stained-glass
windows by Max Ingrand
depicting the life of St-Louis.

TOURS:

Tours has many attractions, from the little old houses in the Place Plumereau and the magnificence of Place Jean-Jaurès.

Founded by the Romans in the first half of the I century A.D. on the left bank of the Loire, near its confluence with the Cher, this town was called *Caesarodunum* and was one of the many settlements established by the emperor Augustus to protect the Roman territories which, at that time, bordered with those of the Gallic population of the Turones. The area selected was subject to flooding, but this did not stop the town developing to such an extent that when, in the III century, it was devastated by a barbaric raid which led to a rapid decline, it boasted three thousand inhabitants, a large temple, an amphitheatre and the new name of *Civitas Turonum*.

After a long period of decline, Tours was reborn as an important religious centre built around its bishops, first and foremost St-Martin, who died here in 397. Conquered first by the Visigoths and then the Merovingians, it flourished under Charlemagne, was sacked by the Normans, and became a hereditary earldom of the d'An-

jou family; it was only reconquered for France by Philippe Auguste in 1204. At the time, the town was actually divided into two clearly distinct poles, Tours itself and the more flourishing suburb of Châteauneuf. It was the Hundred Years' War, with the danger of capture by the enemies of King John II the Good, which led the inhabitants, in 1356, to unite the two settlements within a single walled circuit, thus giving origin to the Tours which in 1461, under Louis XI, became the capital of the kingdom. It was this king who promoted the silk industry in Touraine, destined to become the leading element in the development of the entire region. Thus, until 1540, Tours underwent a period of great economic, artistic, architectural and demographic prosperity. But when, in the XVI century, the Kings of France began to prefer first Blois then Paris as their residence, at the same time as the fighting between Catholics and Protestants began inflicting devastation, the town plunged into a rapid and unstoppable decline, accentuated by the crisis in the silk industry, caused by the revocation of the Edict of Nantes in 1685.

Few events have marked the history of Tours since then, not all of them positive: after the fall of the Second Empire, it was chosen as the seat of a temporary government national defence delegation (1870); the following year it was occupied by the Prussians; in 1940 and 1944 it was seriously damaged by first German and then Allied bombing raids which devastated its architectural and artistic heritage. After the war, the Dorian brothers, architects, proposed a reconstruction plan aimed at respecting and exploiting the existing historical buildings. The economic boom, which began in 1960, brought new life to the town and opened the doors to post-modernist architectural innovations concentrated mainly in the suburbs.

To this day, even the most futuristic innovations do not seem to have been exhausted: the town is still changing its appearance. It is, however, still possible to admire the remains of the **Gallic-Roman town-walls**, the characteristic quarter of the **cathedral of St-Gatien** (XIII-XVI c.), with the abbatial **church of St-Julien**, the **tower of Guise**, the **Châteauneuf quarter**, with the basilica and tomb of St-Martin, the **fountain of Beaune**, the **church of Notre-Dame-la-Riche** (XV-XVI c.), the **Hôtel Gouin**, and the interesting **Museum of Fine Arts** in the ancient archbishopric.

St-Cosme

The ancient hermitage, transformed in the XI century into a priorate under the jurisdiction of St-Martin à Tours, was restored in the XV century by Louis XI and had some illustrious guests: Agnès Sorel, Catherine de' Medici, Henry III and the poet Ronsard, who was commendatory prior and buried here. After the suppression of the priorate, in 1742, the church was demolished, and the other buildings soon fell to an early ruin.

The remains of the priorate of St-Cosme.

Plessis-lès-Tours

The castle of Plessis-lès-Tours is located in the town of La Riche on the outskirts of Tours.
In the XI century a fortress stood between the Loire, the Cher and the Rio Ste-Anne which connected the two rivers. The place was then known as Les Montils. Starting from 1444 Charles VII often stayed there, and had some work done. Louis XI purchased it in 1467 for 5,500 gold écus. Construction and general work on the new buildings and dungeons lasted until 1470. In that year Louis XI brought 17 Italian workmen to the castle to set up the first silk factory in Tours. In the XVIII century the castle was restored, and in 1781 it became a hospice for the poor of Tours. In 1790 it was sold as national property and in 1796 three quarters of it was destroyed. In the XIX century it was used in succession as an ammunitions factory, farm and warehouse. All this naturally caused considerable damage to what was left of the buildings. In the XX century Dr. Chaumier restored it and transformed it into a vaccine factory.

Louis XI is the most important person who stayed at the castle. His confessor, St. Francis of Paola stayed there in 1482. Charles VIII stayed there as did Louis XII who spent a long convalescence there in 1505. The following year, 1506, the Estates General met there and gave him the title of Father of the Country, and decided that Francis of Angoulême (the future Francis I) would marry Claude of France. Charles IX, Catherine de' Medici, and Henry III all stayed there on several occasions. And in 1559 Henry III and Henry of Navarre met in the gardens and sealed their reconciliation. Henry IV developed the silk industry, and planted the first mulberry bushes from Provence. Louis XIII also stayed at the castle; and Sir Walter Scott mentioned Plessis-lès-Tours in "Quentin Durward".

Outside, the remaining portions of the building that were restored during the past two centuries, correspond to the southern portion of the former royal residence made of brick and stone (it served as a model for other castles in the region: Jallanges, Luynes, etc.), however, the remains of the ancient castle are barely recognizable.

Inside, little remains of the original elements. The bedroom known as the Louis XI bedchamber is merely a replica. There is a **museum** dedicated to **St. Francis of Paola**, the hermit monk from Calabria in Italy who founded the order of the Minim Friars and built the first French abbey of his order on the royal estate at Plessis. The garrett rooms are extremely interesting.

The gardens are not kept exceptionally well.

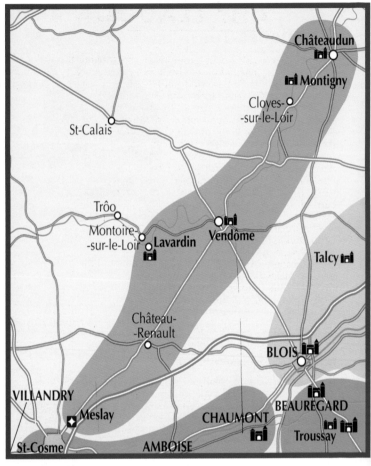

CHÂTEAUDUN

Located on a calcareous promontory overlooking the valley, the château of Châteaudun was built in the X century by the Counts of Blois, to whom it belonged until 1391, when it was bought by Duke Louis d'Orléans along with the entire earldom of Blois and Dunois. In 1439, the château passed to the duke's natural son, John, the *beau Dunois,* famous for heroically fighting against the English alongside Joan of Arc. The property remained in the possession of his descendants until the XVIII century when it was inherited by the Dukes of Luynes. In 1938, it was purchased by the State, which carried out thorough restoration work. What can be admired today is the château "reconstructed" according to the will of the *beau Dunois* by the architect Nicole Duval, and subsequently restructured by the architect Hardouin. Only a majestic circular tower remains of the ancient fortress of the Counts of Blois, alongside which stands the Holy Chapel, built in the XV century.

The Renaissance profile of the château of Châteaudun, and, right, a detail of he famous Dunois Gothic staircase, in richly worked stone, by Nicole Duval.
Preceding page, Montigny.

MONTIGNY 🏰

I mmersed in greenery, richly furnished and still inhabited, the Château of Montigny owes the neo-Gothic appearance of its east façade to the architect Parent, who was commissioned to create it in 1886 by Duke Lévis-Mirepoix. The entire château is the result of complex construction work carried out between 1475 and 1495 by Jacques de Renty, after the previous fortress, built in the XII century, was almost completely dismantled in 1415. Particularly charming is the beautifully tended park which flourishes all around the château and onto which the façade, restored in 1831 by the Prince of Montmorency-Laval, opens.

A view of Vendôme.

VENDÔME 🏰

T he castle of Vendôme stands at the southern boundary of this lovely city of art, in a relatively natural setting.
In 1030 Geoffroi Martel built the first castle-fortress. In 1037 Anne de Bourgogne ordered the construction of the Collegiate Church of St-George inside the castle walls. In the XII century the wooden palisades were replaced by a stone wall and at the same time, the eastern door was built along with the Poitiers tower. In the XVII century César de Vendôme built the access ramp, opened the Beauce gate on the south and erected a long building to the east. The castle became a palace where balls and fêtes were held, but in the XVIII and XIX centuries it gradually fell into ruin. After the death of César de Vendôme in 1665 it remained vacant and the Revolution brought the fatal blow. The castle was the residence of the Counts and Dukes de Vendôme. In 1170 it hosted Henry II

The Beauce gate.

of England, in 1227 Blanche de Castille, and the future King St-Louis, the trial of the Duke d'Alençon in 1458, Francis II and Mary Stuart in 1560, and in the XVII century it was the home of César de Vendôme son of King Henry IV and Gabrielle d'Estrées. Antoine de Bourbon and Jeanne d'Albret, the parents of Henry IV were buried in the Collegiate Church of St-George. Some of the ruined portions are of definite interest. The remains of the first donjon date from the XI century. The Poitiers Tower (XII and XV centuries) still has nearly all its internal structures. The four semicircular towers built on XII century revetments rise above the gardens. The Beauce gate is worthy of admiration. Only the foundations of the Collegiate Church of St-George can be seen. A large romantic garden is the ideal setting for a stroll among the ruins. The view of Vendôme, the Abbey of the Trinity, and the Loire valley are extremely picturesque and invite discovery.

The rectangular tower (XI c.), one of the best preserved remains of the château of Lavardin.

Wall paintings (XII-XV c.) in the nave of the church of St-Genest.

LAVARDIN

The first castle built on this site dates from 1030. As customary in that period, it was made of wood and mud. The castle of Lavardin was the main stronghold of the Counts de Vendôme since the XII century. Because of its location on the border between the holdings of the Capetian Kings of France and the Kings of Anjou, it was to play an important role in many events. In 1188, after having taken Troo and Montoire, Henry II of England and his son, Richard the Lion-Heart, mounted an unsuccessful siege of the castle. In the XV and XVI centuries the buildings were remodeled. In 1589 it was taken

over by the troops of the Catholic League; in 1590 it was besieged and conquered by the Prince of Conti, commander of the forces of King Henry IV. The king, who as Duke de Vendôme owned the castle, ordered it destroyed.

Though severely damaged by the elements, the ruins situated on a plateau above the Loire Valley still give a clear idea of three circles of walls around the small castle (XVI century) and the 26 metre tall rectangular tower (XI century) which was flanked by two equally tall towers in the XII century. The final circle of walls known as the "shirt" is the best preserved. One should not miss the church of St-Genest at the foot of the castle, where there are interesting murals from the XII to XVI centuries.

The XII century bridge that spans the Loire offers a lovely view of the banks and the village.

THE FERME DE MESLAY.

The fortified farm of Meslay, just a few kilometers from Tours, is the last trace of the dense network of settlements created by the monks of the Benedictine Abbey of Marmoutier, founded by St-Martin in 372, to protect their estates. The building also represents one of the most interesting examples of XIII century civil architecture. Built by abbot Hugues de Rochecorbon, long stretches of its ancient boundary walls are still intact today. Its features are quite unmistakeable, there is a central gate protected by an arch sunk deeply into the powerful fortification, surmounted by a building which is both squat and slender, with its roof stretching out in an accentuated verticality and an elegant mullioned window adorning the façade. On the whole, the original structure is excellently preserved: only the chestnut-wood roofing was entirely replaced in the XV century.

Today, the fortification hosts art shows and exhibitions and has also proved to be an excellent auditorium during the *Fêtes musicales de Touraine*, which attract accomplished artists from all over the world.

The rectangular tower overhanging the entrance gate of the Ferme de Meslay.

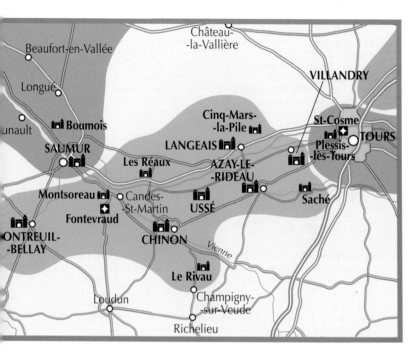

Beaufort-en-Vallée

Longué

Château-
-la-Vallière

VILLANDRY

unault

Boumois

Cinq-Mars-
-la-Pile

St-Cosme

TOURS

SAUMUR

LANGEAIS

Plessis-
-lès-Tours

Les Réaux

AZAY-LE-
-RIDEAU

Montsoreau

Candes-
-St-Martin

USSÉ

Saché

Fontevraud

ONTREUIL-
-BELLAY

CHINON

Vienne

Le Rivau

Loudun

Champigny-
-sur-Veude

Richelieu

Villandry.

CINQ-MARS-LA-PILE 🏰

The castle is situated on a rocky spur in the village of Cinq-Mars-la-Pile (between Tours and Langeais), on the banks of the Loire. In 1230 the St-Médard family began construction of a new castle over the ruins of an older one. In the XIV and XV centuries the Rouge and Châteaugiron families built the buttresses. In the XVI century Louis II de la Trémoïlle, a soldier who participated in the Italian war modernized the castle which, would then be dismantled in the following century. Between 1840 and 1860 Bussiènne, a horticulturist, designed and planted the gardens, demolishing the main portion of the building.

Henri d'Effiat, Marquis of Cinq-Mars, was born in the castle in 1620. He was beheaded at Lyon in 1642, accused of having plotted against Richelieu. With the power of his prose, in "La Conjuration de Cinq-Mars et de Thiou", Alfred de Vigny has raised this castle to unusual importance. Hortense Mancini, Mazarin's niece, lived there as well. During the Revolution the castle still belonged to the famous Luynes family.

Originally, the castle was encircled by walls and four XIII century towers, only two of which remain today. The only other remaining part of the castle is the "salle d'armes" of the King's Master of the Horse (XVII century). The first two floors of the towers have ogival, eight-section arched ceilings. The turret of the large tower, the large square room on the third floor, the double windows and fireplaces are all part of the work done in the XIV and XV centuries. The castle gardens are truly fascinating with their thick woods, intriguing maze, carefully trimmed box hedges and well-laid paths.

LANGEAIS

T hanks to its position on the western side of Tours, on the banks of a river, Langeais was of considerable strategic importance both as a fortress blocking access to the capital of the province as well as an outpost against aggressors from the west. Evidence of this is to be found in the ruins of Fulk Nerra's bastion which date to the X century and which are in what is now the park of the castle.

Only the walls on the east and north are still extant. The other two walls of the bastion, which was in the form of an elongated rectangle, were torn down in 1841.

The castle taken as a whole mirrors the soul of its builder, the fearsome Fulk Nerra, Count of Anjou, nicknamed in his time "The Black Hawk". He was a typical example of the feudal outlaw: ferocious, perfidious and cynical with an insatiable lust for power. At the same time he was endowed with a superstitious piety and was famous for his excesses.

His gifts as strategist and statesman permitted this founder of the Angevin dynasty to continue in power for fifty years.

When, under the reign of Hugh Capet, Fulk took possession of the holdings of Eudes I, Count of Blois and of Tours, he had this fortress built as a point of support at the top of a promontory-shaped hill enclosed by the valleys of the Loire and of the Roumer at their confluence.

After his death, the house of Anjou continued its unrelenting course which was to culminate in 1154 in the consecration as King of England of Henry of Anjou, called Plantagenet. Since this great grandson of William the Conqueror had married Eleanor of Aquitaine,

The drawbridge giving access to the château.

Langeais became one of the outposts of his immense French possessions, which included the lands of the Loire, Normandy and Aquitaine.

The Capetian monarchy at this point cuts a poor figure with regard to its vassal. In the war which followed, it was to be saved by the internal struggles of the Plantagenets which Philippe Auguste skilfully manipulated. Taking advantage of the assassination of the Duke of Bretagne, perpetrated by John Lackland, son of Henry Plantagenet, Philippe Auguste brought the assassin to trial before the court of Paris and, encouraged by his victories, deprived him of his French possessions.

From this moment on Langeais was part of the French royal holdings even though it was ceded various times as guarantee. This was the case in 1218 when the castle passed to Hugues X of Lusignan who had married Isabelle, widow of John Lackland.

In the course of the XIII century, custody of Langeais was entrusted successively to Guillaume des Roches, Hugues Lusignan, Alphonse of France, brother of St-Louis, Pierre de la Brosse, Chamberlain of Philip the Bold who, accused of complicity with the King of Castile who was then at war with France, was hanged at Montfaucon in 1278.

During the Hundred Years' War, Langeais fell into the hands of the English more than once. In 1428 they abandoned it upon receiving ransom, on condition that "the castle be torn down and razed to the ground, except the large tower".

Aware of the need of building a new fortress on this same site, Louis XI entrusted the direction of the works to his personal counselor Jean Bourré, who also held the office of "Captain of Langeais".

Jean Briçonnet, General of Finances, mayor of Tours, was set in charge of payments for the works and construction of the castle of Langeais in 1465 and 1467. With its high walls and its narrow cross-bar windows its three round towers and its encircling wall of machicolations and crenellations, the new building is the perfect picture of an imposing austere fortress. One of the characteristics of this facade is the continuity of the sentinel walk which surrounds the entire building, towers included, for a length of 130 metres, always on the same level. The king's purpose in rebuilding this castle was that of protecting to the west the royal residences of Tours, Plessis-lès-Tours and Amboise, which were vital to his government. To the east they were protected by Chaumont and to the south by Chinon and Loches.

On the 16th of December, 1491, the castle of Langeais was the stage for an event that was to make it more famous than any other castle – the wedding of Charles VIII and Anne de Bretagne, as a result of which Brittany was annexed to France. This union was to throw European politics into confusion. The duchess Anne had already been married by proxy to Maximilian of Austria, Emperor of the Holy Roman Empire, and Charles VIII was engaged to his daughter Margaret of Austria, who with this wedding in mind had been brought up at the court of France. The union had been planned by the regent Anne de Beaujeu who wanted to unite Brittany to the French kingdom and was conscious of the danger of letting it fall into the hands of the Emperor (even if, as Duke of Bretagne, he was a vassal of the king). "Since Charles was of the opinion", says Brantome, "that it was not a good idea to have such a powerful lord in his own realm, he took Anne from Maximilian, her promised spouse, and married her".

The situation had precipitated. Charles VIII did not present himself to the duchess at Rennes, which was besieged by French troops,

A view of the austere but evocative chapel, with its characteristic slender vault and the extreme severity of the furnishings.

The Guards Room, with the monumental fireplace and two bronze light fittings by Dürer in the background.

A detail of the typical Flemish tapestry known as "aux aristoloches" (XVI c.).

until a few days before the ceremony. I order to escape the opposing party, the princess arrived secretly at the castle of Langeais, where the king was waiting for her. This wedding was more like a kidnapping than anything else.

The most important clauses in the wedding contract were the unification of Brittany with France, and, to ensure this union, the obligation on the part of the queen, if the king died before she did and left no heirs, to marry his successor. And this was just what happened. A second marriage made her the wife of Louis XII. The chroniclers of the time have left us fantastic accounts of the pomp and magnificence of the wedding.

After this, Langeais disappears from History with a capital H. As an aside, let it be remembered that Charles IX stayed at the castle on November 19, 1565, and Louis XIII in the early days of October 1627, on the journey which took him to the siege of La Rochelle.

In 1631 the castle, which up to this time had been ceded to various persons only as a pledge (the holder had only the use while the property legally remained in the king's possession), was given to Louise of Lorraine, daughter of the Duke of Guise, who ceded it almost immediately to the Marshal Marquis d'Effiat Baron of Cinq-Mars and father of Louis XIII's favorite, who was beheaded in 1642. In 1765 the descendants of the Marquis d'Effiat ceded it to the Baron of Champchevrier, but it went instead to the Duke of Luynes who exercised his preferential right. The château came through the Revolution intact, and in 1797 it was acquired by a bourgeois of Tours, Charles-François Moisant, who left it in a state of abandon.

Houses were built right against the walls of the castle and the finest hall on the ground floor was transformed into a stable for the gendarmes.

Bought in 1839 by a Parisian lawyer, Christophe Baron, the building underwent radical restoration. Some of this was the work of fantasy, such as the extension of the machicolations to the entire facade of the internal courtyard, or the crenellations which decorated the ridges of the roof.

Jacques Siegfried, who bought the castle in 1886, set about to restructure it fundamentally. The most important aspect was the restoration of the interior, to which he dedicated twenty years of his life.

The unity of style which the castle owed to the speed with which it had been built survived the centuries.

Since the people who had lived there up to 1641 had not been the owners, but had only enjoyed the use of the building, they had not been interested in shouldering the costs of bringing up to date a building which remained the king's property. In the following periods the dimensions and the solidity of the construction probably discouraged any unwarranted desire for changes. While this may have been true of the exterior it was not the case with the inside and Jacques Siegfried, who worshipped the past and took the castle to heart, set out to restore the interior of the monument to what it must have looked like when it was built.

With this end in mind he engaged a talented young architect, Lucien Roy, and the most famous archaeologists such as Palustre, Foulc, Spitzer, Peyre and Bonafé. Their attempts to be as historically exact as possible led them to search particularly for elements of flamboyant Gothic style. The furniture and wood panelling is either authentic or copied from originals. The pavements, which differ from room to room, were designed on examples of the XV century or copied from period paintings. They are the most noteworthy aspect of the restoration, for the furniture, with few exceptions, is all period. Wardrobes, chests, bureaus are either XV century or Renaissance.

But the highlight of the interior decoration is the marvelous collection of XIV and XV century tapestries – over thirty – which Jacques Siegfried put together between 1888 and 1900.

The oldest pieces, including various millefleur and a splendid "Crucifixion", are Flemish, while the others are mostly Aubusson. The greater part date to the XVI century but are still in Gothic style, like the hunt scenes, the story of Nabucodonosor, the curious "Miracles due to the intervention of the Holy Sacrament". The intrinsic value of these works of art, including sculpture and paintings, is intensified by the fact that they harmonize perfectly with the furniture. This inviting and lived-in aspect of the château strikes the visitor in sharp contrast to the forbidding aspect of the fortress from outside.

In 1904 Jacques Siegfried offered to donate the château and his collections to the French Institute. For fear that this example of the national patrimony might be bought by some wealthy art lover from the New World and transported stone by stone to America, the Institute decided to accept the financial burden that maintaining a monument of similar size entailed.

Actually the continuous growth of tourism and the position of Langeais on the route of the châteaux of the Loire were to provide the Siegfried Foundation with the means not only to maintain the monument but also to provide for the periodic restoration required. The French Institute sees to it that its management is completely autonomous, with the aid – for some of the works of restoration – of the Caisse Nationale des Monuments Historiques et des Sites.

In 1924, and again in 1938, Jacques Siegfried's daughter, Agnès, continued her father's work, donating the large park which, beyond the ruins of Fulk Nerra's tower, dominates the valley of the Loire to the west – with the houses which climb up the slopes of the hill – and on the northwest the road that leads to the upland plain.

The monument is thus amply protected on this side. To the east and to the north, the old city embraces the château and provides a suitable environment.

In line with the spirit of the donor and its own principles, the French Institute promises to perservere and continue his work.

VILLANDRY

This elegant Renaissance château stands not far from the Loire and from ancient prehistoric menhirs. Originally a feudal stronghold stood on the spot, where Philippe Auguste King of France and Henry II Plantagenet King of England met on July 4, 1189. Their contrasts were arbitrated in the Medieval tower that still stands in the southwest corner of the castle. Philippe Auguste won out and his victory was then sanctioned by the peace of Azay.

A few centuries later the manor became the property of Jean le Breton president of the Chamber of the Counts of Blois. Minister for Francis I, Jean was charged by the king with controlling the construction of the royal palaces of Fontainebleau and Chambord, since he was well-versed in architecture. For himself, Jean le Breton (whose family originally came from Scotland) set out to build a palace which was just the opposite of the foreboding feudal castle. The older structures, with the exception of the keep, were razed to the ground and in 1536 the construction of a new building with a U-shaped ground plan around a court of honor facing the valley of the Loire was begun. The two large L-shaped wings contain typically Renaissance elements borrowed from the palaces built at the beginning of the XVI century: large windows framed by pilasters with capitals in classic style, horizontal mouldings, large dormer windows decorated with superstructures enhanced by pediments and volutes.

The wide façades were enlivened with slight asymmetries (in the placing of the windows, the length and angle of the wings) and by the arched porticoes on two sides of the courtyard.

Partially surrounded by a moat fed by ground water, the castle was landscaped with large gardens laid out on three different levels.

*The ornamental vegetable gardens which extend
beyond the moat and boast the singular characteristic
of realizing multicoloured flower-beds with
geometrical patterns, using exclusively vegetables
and fruit plants.*

Landscape gardening developed together with the Italian Renaissance and was conceived of as a pendant to the architecture. At the time, Italian style gardens were characterized by a geometric layout and a typically architectonic taste. In France, this new fashion led to the creation of the "French garden", where the garden became larger, eliminating the perimetral walls and limiting the architectural structures in general. Convenient avenues ran along the flower beds where low hedge borders set off the decorative plants.

The gardens of Villandry are perfect examples of this concept – they are all large and are set on various terraces. Water is collected on the topmost level while a middle terrace lies on the same plane as the rooms on the ground floor of the castle (ornamental garden) and a lower level contains the ornamental vegetable gardens. The upper terrace, which extends to a wood of tall trees, consists of orchards criss-crossed by shady paths.

In line with this principle, the entire park of Villandry is cut through by green galleries, placed above the neighboring gardens so that they can be seen from above. The ornamental garden on the middle terrace in the part nearest the castle consists of the so-called "gardens of love". Here four large squares of box shrubs and flowers form motifs which symbolize the allegories of love. The square to the northwest, with its wounded hearts arranged according to the allegory of the ball, indicates passionate love, while the northeast

One of the three buildings enclosing the court of honour, forming a large U-shape. Of particular note are the large dormers and the long arcade.

square with fans, horns and billets-doux (at the center) represents adulterous love, dominated by yellow flowers. Tender love is symbolized in the southwest, with hearts separated by flames of love and by the masks worn for balls, while the last square on the southeast evokes tragic love with sword blades and the blood-red color of duels.

The southernmost part of the garden contains three large diamond-shaped beds enclosing the crosses of Languedoc, Malta and Béarn. Beyond the moat, lower down, the ornamental vegetable gardens lie between the castle and the edge of the town, with the Romanesque church in the corner. This part of the park is unique in the way in which the geometric designs of the large multicolored beds are created exclusively by vegetables and fruit plants. Long ago, in the XVI century, when the first botanic gardens were created, previously unknown plants were introduced from the Americas. Considered rarities, they were planted in the most prestigious gardens in Europe and were carefully tended so that they might adapt to the new climate. This was also what happened in Villandry and the original aspect of the nine large sections of the vegetable garden have been perfectly reconstructed thanks to the initiative of Dr. Joachim Carvallo, who replanted the old gardens in the early 1900s basing his work on drawings by the landscape painter Androuet du Cerceau. Each vegetable garden creates geometrical motifs in which colors are provided by the leaves of cabbages, carrots, beets and lettuce. Apple and pear trees whose branches form lattices define and separate the beds. The gravel paths – like the center of the nine squares – are decorated with small fountains which were originally used for irrigation.

AZAY-LE-RIDEAU

T he château of Azay-le-Rideau is situated on an enchanting bend of the Indre river. Most probably the name Azay derives from the Latin *Asiacus*, the name of the owner of these lands, and the village of Azay dates back to Roman times. In the Middle Ages, thanks to the presence of a small fortress, it stood watch over the local ford over the Indre.

In the XII century the owner was Rideau or Ridel d'Azay, whose fierceness earned him the nickname "Child of the Devil". Henry II Plantagenet expropriated all his lands, but they were later restored, together with the castle, by Philippe Auguste to Rideau's son, Hugues, knight of Turenne, who served the king faithfully in the battle of Bouvines. Later, in the early XV century, the castle seems to have been in the hands of the Duke of Burgundy. When the duke offended the Dauphin Charles (future Charles VII) and his army, a military attack was launched against the stronghold in 1418: the garrison composed of 354 persons was wiped out and the castle and the nearby town were burned down and completely destroyed. After the fire, which left only ruins in its wake, the place was for a time known as Azay-le-Brûlé. The present château was built a century later on the area of the precedent construction.

A historical panorama of the late XV century helps to explain the characteristics of the new building. At that time Charles VIII and Louis XII organized military expeditions to Italy where they were impressed by the art and architecture they found there. As a result many artists and craftsmen were called to France in the employ of the king and his followers.

*The bedroom of Pierre de Filley de la Barre, containing
a four-poster bed with bright floral decorations in silk.*

Their mark is most clearly to be seen in the region of the Loire where the royal court resided from the time of Charles VII on. The Italianate style of the châteaux of Amboise and of the remodelling of the castle of Blois was soon copied in the residences of the old noble families and in those of the aspirant nobility. Gilles Berthelot, the owner of a part of the territory of Azay-le-Rideau at the beginning of the XVI century, was just such a man, an important financier whose father, Martin Berthelot, had been Maître de la Chambre des Finances for Louis XI and Charles VIII.

Gilles, in a brilliant career, became a counselor to the king, Maître de la Chambre des Comptes and mayor of Tours. Thanks to his marriage with Philippa Lesbahy, who owned the rest of the territory of Azay, he was able to reunite the entire estate under one owner and begin construction of the grandiose castle.

With the financial and political backing of various relatives who held important posts, Gilles Berthelot began the reconstruction of the medieval manor in 1518. That summer, under the supervision of master builder Etienne Rousseau, as many as 120 laborers were at work preparing the foundations. What was left of the previous stronghold had to be eliminated and the area then had to be drained before setting up the wooden pilings on which the whole building rests. Cream-colored tuff from the Cher valley was used for the building itself. The blocks were carried on barges as far as Port-aux-Chalands near Vallères and then transported on wagons for the remaining ten kilometers.

The château has an unusual L-shaped ground plan and its architectural details reveal the evolution from the Gothic to the Renaissance style and a new concept of the dwelling which is no longer a stronghold but a pleasant residence. Only an occasional element of military architecture, lightened by a Renaissance imprint, remains side by side with a few aspects that are still' Gothic, like the high-pitched slate roofs. This was due as much to the taste of Philippa, who kept close track of the proceedings and supervised the construction work, conferring an exquisitely feminine touch to the building, as it was to the work of the master builder Rousseau, the sculptor Pierre Maupoint and the carpenter Jacques Thoreau. Balzac, who wrote "Le Lys dans la Vallée" near Azay, described the château in these words: "Coming to the top of the hill I admired for the first time this faceted diamond, inserted in the Indre, mounted on pilasters decorated with flowers".

Seen from the outside, the castle has corner towers set on walls which jut out from the main building and which are linked together on the outside by a sentinel walk. This was built out of respect for the preceding tradition and has no function at all in a castle without an enclosed courtyard. Numerous references to the Italian Renaissance are to be found side by side with elements which imitate the dwellings of the older French nobility. The pilasters with their capitals which support the horizontal cornices, the superstructures of the dormer windows with pediments, volutes and shellshaped clouds, and the overall symmetry reveal an Italianate classicizing inspiration. This is also the case of the staircase of honor, entrance to which is through twin doors surmounted by reliefs of Francis I's salamander and the ermine of Claude of France. The three upper levels of the staircase are characterized by straight flights with landings which lead to the mullioned Italianate loggias which overlook the garden below. The ceilings over the stairs have stone coffering bordered by arches in which the portraits of the XV and XVI century kings and queens were sculpted in the XIX century. The innovation of this staircase makes it one of the key points of French Renaissance architecture – under the stimulus of new concepts, the narrow spiral staircase of medieval origin was abandoned. Broad straight flights of stairs became popular, no longer illuminated by narrow louvers but by large loggias which provide a

The large dance hall, with the elegant Flemish tapestries.

view over the park as well as letting in light. There are various rooms inside the château on the ground floor (the royal room and the red room) as well as more all-purpose rooms and a kitchen. The first floor contains a dining room, a ball room, and a blue room as well as those of Francis I and of Claude of France.

Gilles Berthelot never finished the construction work on the castle. His cousin Semblançay, who was Superintendent of Finances, was accused of having stolen public funds, found guilty, and hanged in Montfaucon. Gilles found himself in a difficult situation and thought it wise to flee while there was still time. In 1527 he sought refuge in the free city of Metz where he died in exile ten years later.

The so-called bedroom of Francis I, where Gothic and Renaissance styles harmonize.

The castle, with all its lands, was confiscated by Francis I and given to the captain of the guards, Antoine Raffin, who carried the work to completion.

Later, when the royal seat was definitively removed to Paris by Francis I, Touraine's importance diminished. The château of Azay-le-Rideau belonged to the families of Cossé de Gonnord, St-Gelais de Lusignan, Vassé. In 1603 a chapel was added, in which the owners of the castle were subsequently buried. In the XVII century the Kings of France only rarely sojourned at Azay. In 1619 the St-Gelais family offered hospitality to Louis XII, while Louis XIV probably sojourned there in 1650. After the building of the annexes at the end of the XVII century (to be used as stables and as servants' quarters), further work was undertaken in 1845 by the Marquis of Biencourt, owner of the château. It was in that year that the right tower of the court of honor, which up till then had still been in the older medieval style, was rebuilt. Twenty years later a second projecting tower was erected in the same style and with the same materials, so as to make one of the facades more symmetrical.

In 1871, after the defeat of the French army, Prussian troops were quartered in the castle which had been requisitioned from the fourth Marquis of Biencourt. In that year, on the 19th of February, Prince Frederick Charles of Prussia with his general staff was housed there. The tale goes that during supper, which was eaten in the kitchen, a heavy chandelier fell from the keystone in the ceiling onto the prince's table and almost killed him. Frederick thought it was an attempt on his life and the officers had a hard time persuading him not to set fire to the castle in retaliation.

The building later once more became the property of the Marquises of Biencourt who sold it in 1904 when the society they administered went bankrupt. The new owner, M. Arteau, sold the château to the State for the sum of 200,000 francs. The building has since been restored while the park and the bend of the Indre again look as they originally did. The rooms inside have been turned into a

Renaissance Museum thanks to the recovery of furniture, tapestries, objects of daily use and paintings. Among the material exhibited, mention should be made of the canopied bed which belonged to the king's marshal, Pierre de Filley de la Barre, who died in the siege of Nice in 1705. This piece of furniture, marked by an animated floral decoration in silk, is in the blue room, while another tester bed with damask, originally in the castle of Effiat, is in the red room. Other pieces of Renaissance furniture in wood furnish the rooms of the castle: the chest in Francis I's room is decorated with small pilasters and with fantastic animals on either side of the two medallions, while in the kitchen is an elegant chest with two profiles carved on the front. The kitchen also contains examples of cupboards and utensils in ceramics and in metal, such as grills, fire tongs, forks, basins and pitchers. The collection of tapestries in Azay-le-Rideau includes the XVI century tapestry of the "Three Fates" executed in Brussels, which is on exhibit in the ballroom near another tapestry of the same period with plant motifs.

On the other walls of this room are four large XVII century tapestries of Flemish production with biblical scenes such as the "Reconciliation of Esau and Jacob", the "Judgement of Solomon", the "Ark of the Covenant", and the "Visit of the Queen of Sheba to Solomon". In the dining room on the ground floor are XVI century Flemish tapestries with the "Queen Semiramis", the king's messenger and "Balthazar's feast". The tapestries in the royal chamber, designed by Simon Vouet, represent the "Love story of Rinaldo and Armida". The two tapestries with the palaces of Vincennes and Versailles, in the blue room, come from the Lille workshop, while those with hunting scenes come from Beauvais. To make the museum more complete, these rooms also contain numerous paintings with the portraits of the Kings of France and members of the royal family, including Francis I, Henry II, Catherine de' Medici, Francis II, Charles IX, Henry III, Margaret of Valois and Louis XIV.

The salamander, symbol of Francis I, stands out on the monumental fireplace in the room named after the king.

SACHÉ

The castle of Saché is located 6 km from Azay-le-Rideau on the way to Montbazon.

It was built between the end of the XV and the beginning of the XVI century, over the foundations of a small, XII century manor. In the XV century it was owned by the Rousseley family. In the XVIII century it was transformed, and specifically a large staircase was built. In the XIX century, the owner De Margonne transformed the castle: he had the window mullions removed and suspended ceilings installed in all the rooms.

Honoré de Balzac lived at the De Margonne's castle, intimate friend of M. de Margonne's mother, and father of his step-brother and it was there that he wrote many of his famous novels: "Louis Lambert", "Le Père Goriot" (Father Goriot), "La Recherche de l'Absolu" (The Quest of the Absolute); "Les Illusions Perdues", (Lost Illusions); "César Birroteau", and "Le Lys dans la Vallée", (The Lilly of the Valley) in which one can read descriptions of the Indre valley from Saché to Pont-du-Ruan.

On the outside, this XVI century manor house still has one of its original XII century towers. A new tower was built in the XVIII century with a straight inside staircase that replaced the XVI century spiral steps. Inside, the rooms were redone in the XIX century to make them more comfortable. In the salon, the dining-room and Balzac's bedroom there is wallpaper from 1803 that has been carefully restored or remade. The entire suite has been made into a very interesting **Balzac Museum**.

USSÉ

The castle of Ussé, on the edge of the forest of Chinon, stands on an area that was already occupied in ancient times, as shown by the remains of tumulus tombs found nearby. The fort that was built here in the Middle Ages was square in plan with towers and belonged to the descendants of Guilduin de Saumur. In the XV century, when the royal seat was in Chinon, the castle belonged to Jeanne, daughter of the king and of Agnès Sorel, his mistress. When Jeanne married Antoine de Bueil, other towers and architectonic elements were added to the dwelling.

Jean III de Bueil, Jean IV who fell at Azincourt, and Jean V known as "the scourge of the English", courageous warrior in Normandy and Admiral of France, all lived at Ussé. They built the XV century part of the castle, including the external facades, in various stages. When Charles VII died, the Bueil family fell into disgrace: Jean V openly rebelled and sided with the League. In 1485 he ceded the castle to the house of Espinay, a noble Breton family which restructured the complex, as did the Valentinay family later.

The new Renaissance influences caused the new owners to tear down the wing which shut out the panorama towards the valley and to change the aspect of the façades. The interiors were also rebuilt and lower ceilings were installed. The Renaissance chapel in the park was built between 1520 and 1538 by Charles d'Espinay and his wife Lucrezia de Pons. Other works later involved the part of the castle which opened onto the court of honor and the side towards the valley where an Italianate pavilion overlooking the terraced gardens was realized.

A royal chamber was prepared inside the palace in case the king should come for a visit, although as chance would have it he never did. After the Revolution, which left the castle untouched, Ussé passed into the hands of the Duchess of Duras, Claire de Kersaint, who formed a literary circle here, then into the hands of the Countess of Rochejacquelin and finally into those of the de Blacas family, to whose descendants it still belongs. The particularly elegant, fairy-tale-like appearance of this castle at the edge of a dark, mysterious forest seems to have influenced Charles Perrault's conception of the castle in his "Sleeping Beauty".

The castle, still flourishing and lived in, contains a great number of furnishings of great historical value: the royal chamber looks as it did in the XVIII century, while an antechamber contains a valuable XVI century Italian cabinet with intarsias.

The gallery on the ground floor has a collection of weapons and various Flemish tapestries, while other tapestries from Brussels are exhibited in the drawing room. Numerous paintings and pottery are to be seen at Ussé as well as a majolica "Virgin and Child" by Luca della Robbia.

CHINON

T his château, with its close ties to the history of France, was built for the first time in stone in 954 by Theobald I, Count of Blois, on a steep plateau. The stronghold, which replaced a lighter wooden structure, then passed to the rival Count of Anjou, Geoffroi Martel, in 1044.

The Count of Anjou was the first to join the walls of the two original defensive structures (the castles of Milieu and of Coudray) as well as adding towers and the chapel of St-Melanie. The far east wing was added by Henry II Plantagenet, who descended from the Counts of Anjou and the King of England; he called it "St. Georges's fort" dedicating it to the English patron saint. Until 1205 he and his descendants continued construction work, adding the fortress to the east and the internal chapel, the mill tower and the numerous reinforcement towers.

With the beginning of the long war with France, the English stronghold passed under the crown of Philippe Auguste in June of 1205 after a months-long siege. Reconstruction was immediately begun on the towers of the Guards and of the Dogs, the new walls and the large moat which separates the western and the central blocks. Additions continued to be made up to the XV century when the

A cylindrical tower and the Clock tower.

royal apartments and the great throne room were realized. The castle also included prisons where the Knights Templar, whose order had fallen in disgrace, were enclosed in 1308. The dauphin Charles made Chinon his residence. Excluded by the English, he became the "King of Bourges" and received Joan of Arc here in 1429.

The story is told of how Charles mingled with the nobles and had another person take his place. Notwithstanding, Joan recognized him in the crowd and unhesitatingly went up to him saying "Kind Dauphin, the King of Heaven asks that you be crowned at Reims and that you take Orléans..." After having assured himself that the young woman was neither mad nor possessed by the devil, Charles followed her advice and became Charles VII, defeating his adversaries. Chinon thus became the seat of the royal government. The Queen Mary of Anjou and Charles' mistress Agnès Sorel lived here with the king. Their apartments were connected to his by an underground passage. From Chinon Charles VII reorganized France, abolishing the feudal organization, and under his reign the castle lived its moments of greatest splendor; after which it was abandoned by the court. Even so it was at Chinon that Louis XII received Cesare Borgia who had been sent by pope Alexander VI to annul the marriage of the King of France with Jeanne, who was lame and hunchbacked. Once this was done Louis XII was free to marry Anne de Bretagne, widow of Charles VIII.

The château later belonged to Cardinal Richelieu, who left the stronghold to his descendants. At this point the ravages of time were augmented by man-made devastation. In 1699 the Duke of Richelieu demolished Charles VII's throne room and other structures considered passé.

Neglect then led to the collapse of the roofs and pavements, while various towers fell into ruin. The stones were sold as building material. After having risked total demolishment in 1854, the château has been patiently restored: the floors in the royal apartments have been recreated according to their original design and the rooms have been furnished with copies of antique furniture.

133

LE RIVAU

The castle is located at the far end of the village of Lemère, south of Chinon.

The castle's origins date from the XII-XIV century, but there are no documents that can tell us its history. In the XV century ownership passed to the Beauvau family. In that period it was a stark, bare fortress surrounded by moats that framed the cylindrical corner towers. In 1442 Pierre de Beauvau obtained permission from King Charles VII to fortify the castle and made the changes that one can still see today. In the XVIII century the moats were filled in and the west wing was torn down to open the main courtyard to the outside (as at Chaumont, Luynes, Ussé). In the XIX century the superb Gothic chapel on the north side was destroyed, and only a few traces remain. In the XX century the moats were drained and the rooms were restored to their original state.

From the outside, one enters via the tower-gate and the drawbridge which are the most spectacular and most respresentative elements of the XV century defensive fortifications. The façade overlooking the courtyard is a blend of charm and harmony, with its Renaissance decorations. Inside, on the ground floor, there are interesting French-style ceilings and stone floors. The floor tiles on the upper storey are Renaissance "cotto". The furniture also dates from the Renaissance. Note the studded leather wedding chest that has always been in the castle.

The polychromed tombs of the Plantagenets.

The Abbey of Fontevraud.

FONTEVRAUD▪

The Abbey of Fontevraud, one of the most evocative monastery complexes in the whole of France, was founded in 1101 by the hermit Robert d'Abrissel, who wanted to set up a mixed community. The abbey thus separately united in five different buildings (true and proper autonomous convents) monks and lay brothers, nuns, sick people, lepers and repentant public sinners, all under the authority of an abbess. The order enjoyed rapid and constant fortune, also due to the fact that the abbesses, generally from important families, were able to procure influential protection for the abbey. The Plantagenet kings and queens chose to be buried here, in the abbatial church (Henry II, Eleanor of Aquitaine, Richard Lion-Heart and Isabel d'Angoulême). Young men from noble families abandoning the world found refuge in the abbey, and the four daughters of Louis XV were educated here until revolutionaries suppressed the order in 1789. Transformed into a prison by Napoleon, the abbey remained as such until 1963. Today it hosts conferences, seminars, concerts and exhibitions, thanks to an ambitious plan for the recovery and use of its structures. Particularly charming, to this day, in addition to the church in typical Aquitaine style, is the kitchen complex with its numerous chimney-tops and diamond point cut stone roof.

MONTSOREAU 🏰

Today the château of Montsoreau stands a few meters from the banks of the Loire. When it was built in the XV century, the waters of the river lapped its front. In 1820 the embankments were widened. For Jean de Chambes, the builder and an important personage in the court of Charles VII, it served as a point from which to control the various routes which crossed the area, including that of the pilgrims on their way to the Abbey of Fontevraud.

The most famous figure in the history of the castle is without doubt Charles de Chambes immortalized in "La Dame de Monsoreau" by Alexandre Dumas père. Written three centuries after the facts to which it refers took place, the tale was based on the story of Charles, his wife Françoise (and not Diane) and the latter's lover, the lord of Bussy. Françoise de Méridor had taken as her second husband Charles, the Duke of Alençon's chief hunter, who, in spite of the tale, was not old but about the same age as his wife and quite handsome. In the castle of Coutancière, Françoise de Méridor met Louis de Clermont d'Amboise, lord of Bussy and favorite of the Duke of Alençon. He is remembered as being "handsome, with a fine face, clear eyes, a commanding, often seductive, glance" and as a courageous and cultured warrior, a reader of Plutarch. His figure and his often unscrupulous attitudes made him various enemies, and in 1579 the lord of Bussy decided to retire to his estate and left the court. This was when he courted the lady of Montsoreau. He boasted of his success – whether or not – it corresponded to the truth in a letter to a friend at court, to whom he wrote, "I have caught the master hunters deer in my nets". The rumor soon reached the ears of De Chambes, who hurried to the castle and forced his wife, who professed her innocence, to write a note to her

presumed lover inviting him to a tryst in the castle of Coutancière. The mortal trap had been sprung. Louis de Bussy showed up at the appointment with only one friend and as soon as he entered the castle the doors were blocked to prevent his escape. Attacked by a dozen men, he defended himself to his last breath and as about to throw himself out the window he was killed. The ending of the tale is much more prosaic than expected, for his death was received with indifference by Françoise de Méridor who, reconciled with her husband, presented him with several children.

Inside the castle, sixteen rooms host the permanent exhibit "Les imaginaires de Loire," a striking audiovisual itinerary recounts life in the Loire valley. Designed to arouse emotions in visitors of all ages, evocative images and plays of light and music recreate the ancient and present-day look of the river and urge the visitor to explore themes linked to its history and economy—not to mention the many legends associated with the Loire and the castle of Montsoreau.

LES RÉAUX 🏯

Just a few kilometers from Bourgueil, in a fertile valley covered by green vineyards, from the grapes of which excellent red wines are obtained, and where the poet Ronsard loved to stay, there is a characteristic and charming château, Les Réaux. Built at the end of the XV century, the name is linked mainly to its famous eighteenth century owner, Tallemant des Réaux who, with his "Historiettes", traced an amusing and accurate portrait of French society at that time.

On approaching the château, the extreme care taken in its superb ornaments is most striking. The pavilion giving access to the château, in particular, with the two imposing towers flanking it, undoubtedly constitutes its main and rather special embellishment, almost a singular but charming visiting-card. There is an unmistakeable decorative check pattern alternating stone and brick, refined by the presence of elegant sculptural elements, including the salamander, one of the symbols of the Loire valley, which dominates the entrance gate. However, the whole château, with its classical sloping roofs, towers, and large windows opening onto the sturdy walls, represents a place of great charm, a pleasant destination for an interesting visit.

MONTREUIL-BELLAY

L ike many other castles of the Loire, Montreuil was also built on
the orders of the Count of Anjou, Fulk Nerra. This XI century
warrior was a tireless builder and he had the castle set on a steep
slope where it would be easier to deferd.
The manor was given by Fulk to a vassal, Berlay (or Bellay), who
gave his name to the location. Montreuil seems to be derived from
the Latin *Monasteriolum* with reference to the small monastery the
Du Bellay had built near the stronghold. Du Bellay I was followed
by a long line of descendants: the tale is told of how during a hunting expedition near Brossay, Du Bellay I was charged by a large
boar. Without weapons, which he had left lying on the ground, Du
Bellay was about to fall under the tusks of the animal when he
invoked "St-Hubert! St-Hubert!" and succeeded in putting the animal to flight. Because of the prodigious event the Du Bellay family
from then on used the motto "Hubert! Hubert!" as its battle cry.
At that time the castle consisted of a tall main tower surrounded by
moats, and a double circle of walls protected by barbicans. Around
1150, this layout turned out to be essential in resisting sieges when
the Plantagenet King of England moved against the Du Bellay. All
of them, particularly Giraud Du Bellay, had opposed the Counts of
Anjou, who repaid them by sacking the valley of the Thouet and
laying siege to the castle.
After a few months, despite the destruction of the walls, the siege
slackened and the situation ended in a stalemate. The besieged had
sought refuge in the main tower, impregnable thanks to the moats,
and here blessed with the use of a mill, a well and an oven, they
were able to resist for a long time. More-over, subterranean passages
permitted the Du Bellay to communicate with the fort of La Mothe-
Bourbon, while another underground passage, leading north, may
have passed under the Thouet and surfaced near the Abbey of As-

nières. In the end the Count of Anjou won out and the keep was semi-destroyed. The victory was accompanied by a sinister prediction made by the prior of Brossay, who warned him of his imminent death. And indeed, shortly thereafter, he took a bath in the waters near Château-du-Loir, because of the great heat, and came down with a fever which killed him in a few days, during which he refused confession even as he was dying. Giraud Du Bellay, who survived the fall of the castle, also died soon thereafter and in 1155 was buried in the church near the Abbey of Asnières which he had built. Despite the fact that this building was devastated by the Huguenots, a magnificent XIII century choir still exists.

The music room with XVIII century furnishings.

One of the most illustrious descendants of the Du Bellay family was Guillaume Du Bellay, a warrior and governor of Turin and Piedmont who used a network of informers spread throughout the courts of Europe in explicating his diplomatic activity. His brother Jean was also active in this field. As a cardinal he lived at length in Rome with his nephew Joachim. The latter, a subtle poet, left us his sense of nostalgia for his country and for the buildings in the Loire valley in some of his verses: "I like best the dwellings built by my ancestors... I like sharp slate more than hard marble".

The new lords of Montreuil, the Melun-Tancarville and the d'Harcourt, built the defenses of the city in the XV century with a circle of walls and gates of which only four are still to be seen: Porte du Moulin, Porte St-Jean, Porte de Boële and Porte Neuve.

Thanks to the testament and the money of the d'Harcourt, the castle of Montreuil-Bellay received its present aspect.

The entrance consists of the Châtelet, in the area of the older buildings, followed by the Petit-Château (with four apartments meant for the canons of the chapter) and the Château-Neuf. A square building with low ogee arches, situated in an internal court between the Petit-Château and the Château-Neuf, contains the enormous kitchen. A walkway connects this room to the Château-Neuf, with its fine internal staircase which the Duchess of Longueville mounted on horseback. Besides the chapel, with its fine frescoes, the base of a pyramid, whose purpose is still a mystery, is to be found in the castle – at the base of the western towers of the fort.

FROM SAUMUR TO ANGERS

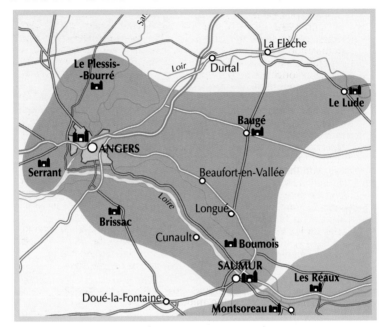

SAUMUR

Once upon a time there was a lovely castle, a vacation residence, so beautiful that René of Anjou, the poet king, chose this above all others as the Castle of Love in his romance "Le Coeur d'Amour Epris..."

"The four walls of this lovely castle were of crystal and at the top of each corner there was a large tower made of ruby stones, fine and resplendent, the smallest of which was larger than the body of a man. And these towers were covered with platinum, as thick as the palm of a hand, and the constructions between these towers were covered with fine gold tiles, exquisitely enameled with the motto of the God of Love – 'A coeur volage...' And to make things even clearer, this lovely castle looked just like château of Saumur in Anjou which lies along the river Loire".

Thereafter various buildings arose on the emerald rock: one built by Thibault le Tricheur, Count of Blois, and later taken over by the terrible Count of Anjou, Fulk Nerra; and one built by Geoffroi Plantagenet of which remains may still exist at the base of the southeast wing. But the story of the present castle begins with the one built by St-Louis.

Saumur belonged first to the Counts of Blois, then to the house of Anjou and then to the King of France. In 1203 Philippe Auguste, rival of the Plantagenets, took over the castle and incorporated it and the territory it controlled into the royal possessions.

Historians place the construction of a fortress at Saumur between 1227 and 1230, when Blanche of Castile was queen regent. The fortress was to serve the Crown in reconquering Angers and that part of Anjou which it had just lost under the Treaty of Vendôme.

Its usefulness from a military point of view lasted only two years, for Angers once more became the royal seat and St-Louis constructed an enormous fortress there which is still standing.

His castle at Saumur was in the shape of an irregular square with a round tower at each corner and it was approximately oriented towards the four cardinal points. The south tower and the west tower still retain almost all of their foundations, dating to the XIII century, and the original six-ribbed vaulting on the ground floor. The east tower, with its more elaborate vaults and keystone decorated with the Anjou coat of arms, was restructured externally.

Not until the second half of the XIV century was the elementary building of the time of St-Louis transformed into a vacation residence under Louis I of Anjou, second son of King John I, who received Anjou in appanage in 1360 before it was transformed into a duchy.

Louis I did not destroy the fortress his ancestor had built, but he did transform it. He used the same ground plan with the round towers as foundations for polygonal towers with high buttresses which supported the sentinel walks of the crenellated machicolations.

The entrance tower as it looks now with its projecting guardhouses appears in the miniature of the month of September in the "Très riches heures du Duc de Berry".

We know that "good King René", grandson of Louis I of Anjou, had sung the praises of Saumur as a Castle of Love and had left his mark on it.

The accounts and diaries of his director of works, preserved in the National Archives, reveal that the construction work on the castle must have been important

Horse Museum: the Saumur cavalry school in an etching by Victor Adam.

to judge from the time involved (from 1454 to 1472) and the cost. Still extant parts dating to the time of King René include two small vaulted rooms in the square tower next to the large tower, the oratory on the first floor with coats of arms carved on the keystone, and "the corridor which leads from the staircase to the tower", with love-knots carved on the keystone presumably in honor of Jeanne de Laval who married in 1454.

At the death of King René, in 1480, the duchy of Anjou returned to the Crown and the castle of Saumur came to house a royal garrison. A century later the Reformation modified the destiny of the castle: King Henry III was forced to ask the King of Navarre for help in saving his throne and concluded a truce with him. With the Treaty of Tours, he ceded Saumur, where there were many Protestants. The future Henry IV named his ambassador and friend, Philippe Duplessis-Mornay, who was in charge of the negotiations, as military governor general.

On April 15, 1589, Duplessis-Mornay entered Saumur and installed his garrison. The next day the King of Navarre in turn entered the city, extremely satisfied to have taken over this key site on the Loire. He ordered the new governor to fortify the fortress "with all diligence and without trying to economize" and left him Bartholomeo, his engineer, to plan and follow the works. In addition to the fortifications around the city, he had built the projecting walls and bastions which still surround the castle and are faced in cut stone. Unfortunately, this wall has lost most of its projecting look-out towers which kept the protruding corners of the bastions under surveillance.

When he arrived in Saumur, Duplessis-Mornay and his family went to live in a "town house" at number 45 Grande Rue, which at the time was quite new and comfortable, for the "castle was all in ruins". However, in 1596, after "some of the inhabitants of the town had attempted to kidnap him and make him leave the place", he decided to move to the stronghold which he first had to repair at great cost to make it habitable.

A man of war and a shrewd diplomat, Duplessis-Mornay was also a learned theologian. In 1593 he founded a Protestant Academy in Saumur which was to bring fame to the city for almost a hundred years. Governor of Saumur for 32 years, he was a faithful servant of the Crown under two kings. Despite this, in 1621 he fell into disgrace when Louis XIII replaced him with a Catholic governor.

The political and military role of the castle thus came to an end. From then on, it began a less glorious epoch. For almost two centuries the old fortress, whose buildings were abandoned and gradually fell into ruin, was used as a gilded prison for various harebrained individuals or gentlemen of rank who had been imprisoned by the king. Their treatment was anything but harsh. Accompanied by a valet or a more important following, they were often allowed to go out into the city. The king's lieutenant in command of the fort frequently invited them to his table.

In 1768 the Marquis de Sade lived at the castle for a fortnight before being imprisoned at Pierre-Encise (near Lyon). Admiral de Kerguélen-Trémarec, explorer of the Indian Ocean, served four years imprisonment here (1774-1778) after he had returned from an unlucky expedition condemned for having abandoned a ship at sea. In 1779, during the American War of Independence, 800 English prisoners were enclosed in the manor as well as in the chapel of the building on the square and in other "annexes" on the bastions. Most of these were sailors as can be gathered from the graffiti they left, in which their names and the date of their capture are often accompanied by the image of a ship.

New works of restoration began in 1811 and ended in 1814. This is undoubtedly when the galleries in the northeast wing were divided up into cells, since the engineer in charge of the works had been told to keep in mind the fact that "in a prison it is necessary to have the greatest possible number of isolated rooms, leaving only a few in common for those persons who were not lucky enough to have a room all to themselves". The prison had just begun to function well when the provisory government ordered all the prisoners to be freed. In 1889 its status as a military building changed and a few years later it became a historical monument. Up until the end of the XIX century, Dr. Peton, mayor of Saumur, had thought of transforming it into a museum. His dream became reality in 1906 when the city bought the château from the State for the incredibly low sum of 2,500 francs and decided to begin restoration, sharing the costs with the Fine Arts Administration. Large carved windows, the remains of great fireplaces, the stained-glass windows of the chapel, and glazed tiles under the earth fills were all brought to light. In particular, a coin with the effigy of Louis XIV provided an approximate date for the castle's transformation into a prison. It is however obvious that the XX century restoration, even though rigorously carried out, could not reproduce the sculptured decoration of the doors and windows and of the fireplaces with the magnificence they must have had in the XIV century.

In 1912 the first floor of the northeast wing, as well as the two towers which flank it, were allotted to the **Municipal Museum**, while the second floor is dedicated to the recently created **Horse Museum**.

BOUMOIS ⬛

S haded by big trees, close to the road, and just a few kilometers from Saumur, the castle of Boumois, feudal in its outward appearance, actually conceals an elegant Renaissance home. René de Thory, lord of the land, rebuilt most of the ancient castle around 1515. In 1760 it was the birthplace of Aristide Dupetit-Thouars who died a hero's death in the battle of Abukir in 1798 after having refused to lower the flag of his ship "Le Tonnant".

From the outside the castle appears to be a fortified enceinte protecting the main courtyard that is reached through a monumental portal. The manor house, flanked by two towers with machicolations is reached by a polygonal turret (the door has a fine Renaissance lock). From the ground up to the top, the dormers and bays are decorated with buttresses and twisted columns. A XVII century dovecot near the main entrance houses a spiral staircase and 1800 compartments. Inside, the big hall on the first floor contains a fine collection of XV and XVI century weapons. On the second floor one can admire a room with a wood ceiling, the guards' walk and a XVI century chapel with a marble statue of Margaret of Savoy and a "Virgin" by Salviati.

BAUGÉ

The charming town of Baugé was founded at the beginning of the XI century by Fulk Nerra and, four hundred years later, it became one the favourite places visited by Yolanda of Aragon and her son, René of Anjou, titular King of Naples. The cousin and brother-in-law of the King of France, Charles VIII, was an extremely well educated prince, loved for his valour and gentle nature, which led to him being called René the Good. In 1455, he began to personally supervise the building work on the château of Baugé: with the simple and essential but elegant linearity of its shapes, it is charming and particularly bright, thanks to the many windows opening onto the façades. René of Anjou often stayed in this pleasant residence, located near woods rich in game and ideal for hunting, and the decorations in the various rooms on the first floor, reached by an elegant staircase, still recall him, with the coat of arms of the Sicilian Anjou family alternating with stars, angels and symbols of Christ's Cross. It is not a coincidence that in the chapel of a nearby hospice, a relic of the True Cross, known as the "Cross of Anjou", is venerated. The château, the right wing of which also contains an interesting oratory, today hosts a large museum with collections of precious examples of weapons, armour and ancient coins.

LE LUDE

The first castle to be built here, known at the time as *Castellum Lusdi*, was in wood as was customary in the Middle Ages. It was part of the property of the Counts of Anjou and was rebuilt in stone in the times of Fulk Nerra. A legend narrates that this was when the Loire was canalized and its course was deviated several kilometers to bring it closer to the castle, while the old river bed became a brook. Another legend of the same period refers to the fact that in the X century a demon inhabited the castle. In the guise of a servant he attempted to kill the owner. It was necessary to call in a bishop, Breviliguet, who used exorcisms to get rid of Satan's emissary.

Remodelling in the XIII century gave the fort a keep with walls, six towers and a deep moat. All that is left today of these structures is a subterranean vaulted room.

This defensive outpost on the Loire was acquired by the Vendôme family in 1378, but they abandoned it in the face of the relentless pursuit of the English troops under the count of Warwick. In 1427 the stronghold was reconquered by Amboise de Loré and Gilles de Rais. Despite the fact that he was a Marshal of France, the latter was unable to escape the gallows after having been condemned for satanic rites.

The new owner from 1477 on, Jean II Daillon, sided with the faction that opposed the French dauphin. After Louis XI became king he pursued Jean for a long time and forced him to hide for seven years in a cave. Reconciled with the king, Daillon obtained important offices in court and was able to turn his attentions to transforming of the castle into a building with three arms around a central court of honor. The work of renovation was completed by Jean II's two successors, both of whom were valorous soldiers. Louis XII's wing, Francis I's wing and the gardens laid out on the area of the old moat were thus added on to Le Lude. Other transformations took place in the following centuries, such as the addition of a monumental facade towards the Loire, in Louis XVI style.

BRISSAC

Once upon a time numerous windmills stood in the Brissac area, close to Angers. During the Carolingian period a local miller who used to rob wheat by making holes in his clients' sacks was given the nickname of *Brêche-Sac*, which was later transformed into the present day name of Brissac. Fulk Nerra, the Count of Anjou, built a Medieval castle as a military stronghold on the site and up until 1434 the various owners were all warriors. The castle was then bought by Pierre de Brézé, an important figure in the royal court who was a minister both under Charles VII and under Louis XI, and who had the building modified. The only thing that remains of this period are the two cylindrical corner towers clearly Gothic in style.

In 1502 (some say 1492) René de Cossé acquired the castle and the surrounding land. Rumor has it that Jacques de Brézé suddenly sold it as the result of the double assassination of his wife Charlotte and her lover, of which he himself was to blame. According to certain legends, the châtelaine's ghost still haunts the castle. The religious wars had in part damaged the dwelling and it was finally transformed in 1614 by Charles II de Cossé, who held the office of Marshal of France. He turned to the well-known architect Jacques Corbineau, who designed an ambitious building for his patron. As planned, it would have been unique for its times, with seven or

A partial view of the Guardroom, wich is 32 metres long.

eight floors, unusually high for buildings in the beginning of the XVII century.

Work was carried out on the central part of the old building, the towers of which were saved, until 1621. This was when death overtook Charles II, who had adhered to the Catholic League and as a faithful follower of Henry IV had opened the gates of Paris to him. The work came to a halt and the castle remained lower than planned and was roofed at this lower level.

The influence of Italian Renaissance art which had already made itself felt in other castles in the region of the Loire is also clearly visible here. The facades, which face the town of Brissac on one side and the park around Aubance on the other, are oriented to the east and to the north, and even though they are elegant, they lack symmetry. Tall chimneys abound on the steep slate roofs while the windows on the façades are surmounted by triangular or arched pediments, both complete and broken.

It was here that on the 12th of August, 1620, Louis XIII was reconciled with his mother Marie de' Medici, Henry IV's widow, and for the occasion the Duc de Cossé organized great celebrations. The reconciliation, in the presence of representatives of the French clergy, took place in the room of Judith after the rebel troops had been driven from Ponts-de-Cé.

In the following centuries the castle continued to belong to the Cossé family, which vaun4ted one of the most illustrious traditions of nobility in France. The family includes four marshals, a grand master of the artillery, five governors of Paris and many other men of state.

The apartments of the castle, lined with sculpted decoration and with richly painted beams and crossbeams on the ceilings, still contain a quantity of antique furniture and decorations. The room of Judith mentioned above contains fine polychrome tapestries and an elegant mantlepiece; the large guardroom is decorated with other tapestries as well as with military curios such as saddles and suits of armor. The dining-room has a monumental staircase with two converging flights of stairs in Louis XIII style. The various rooms also contain many paintings by well known painters which portray the members of the family. The Gothic tower on the south side, part of "a new castle half built on an old castle and half destroyed" (as the Duc de Cossé said regarding his residence) contains a private chapel with a marble low relief by David d'Angers, a local sculptor who worked in the first half of the XIX century.

Room of Judith, where Louis XIII was reconciled with his mother, Marie de' Medici.

MONTGEOFFROY

This beautiful château, located twenty-four kilometers east of Angers, was rebuilt in the 18th century by the Marquis de Contades, Maréchal de France under Louis XV, on the site of a pre-existing castle purchased by his family a century earlier. The façade is framed by two round towers from the original 15th century construction.
In the interior are the original decorations and furnishings of the de Contades family, which still holds title to Montgeoffroy.

SERRANT

In the XIV century the estate of Serrant belonged to the Le Brie family, but the building that existed at the time was only later transformed into the castle we see today. Louis XI granted Pontus Le Brie permission to create a stronghold on this spot, furnished with all kinds of defensive works.

Work began in 1546, under Charles Le Brie, who called in the famous architect Philibert Delorme, the designer of the wing of Chenonceau so daringly suspended over the Cher.

Extremely symmetrical and stylistically unified, despite the fact that the construction work continued throughout the XVI and XVII centuries, the castle of Serrant clearly displays the influence of Renaissance art, like all the luxurious châteaux of the Loire from the time of Francis I on.

The new Renaissance models (wide windows, pilasters, pediments, innovations of great elegance such as the domed roofs of the angle towers) harmonize perfectly with various archaic aspects (the corner towers, the symmetrical layout, the presence of deep moats filled with water).

This is all quite evident in the magnificent façade. Note should be made first of all of the sense of color displayed by the use of shale and tuff, which create an elegant medley of brown and beige under the light line of the dormer windows and the dark slate roof. The double entrance is surmounted by a central body with windows and pilasters, on top of which is a sort of edicule with a triangular

The bedroom prepared in 1808 for Napoleon, with a bust of the Empress Marie Louise, by Canova, on the fireplace.

pediment. At the sides, rows of windows let light into the rooms of the castle, which is now thought of in terms of comfort and beauty. On the top floor the powerful corner towers are completely surrounded by a long balcony. They are roofed by two curious helmet-shaped domes which attempt to go beyond the older method of conical roofing. The upper hemisphere of each dome is surmounted by a lantern with a smaller, analogous, hemispherical roof. Stone bridges with arches supported by pilasters which terminate in pyramids lead over the wide moat at the side into the internal court.

While these structures were being built, the owners of the castle – after the Le Brie family – were the Duke of Montbazon Hercule de Rohan (around 1596) and then from 1636 on, the future Count of Serrant, Guillaume de Beutru. A member of the parliament of Rouen when he was only 22, he was then intendent for Touraine and selector of the king's ambassadors and court counselor. He is remembered for his polished wit, his salacious sense of satire and as a member of the Académie Française as well as for his activities as a diplomat and ambassador. One of his heirs was his granddaughter Margaret, whose husband, Marquis of Vaubrun and lieutenant general of the King's army, fell in the battle of Altenheim in 1675. In memory of her consort, Margaret had the chapel built on the extension of the right wing, on which Jules Hardouin-Mansart, who had already created the Gallery of Mirrors in the castle of Versailles, worked. A monumental tomb for the marquis was built inside, executed by the sculptor Coysevox on a design attributed to Charles Le Brun.

Thereafter the castle of Serrant belonged to an Irish nobleman, Antoine Walsh, and, after 1830, to the Duke of Trémoïlle, to whose descendants it still belongs. Inside the château are magnificent furnishings, including tapestries of Brussels manufacture in the library (with thousands of books) and two busts by Antonio Canova of the Empress Marie Louise. Also worthy of note are the interior staircase, the dining-room and the ground floor ceilings, decorated with coffering.

The chapel contains a polychrome relief with a "Pietà" in addition to the mausoleum of the Marquis of Vaubrun.

PLESSIS-BOURRÉ

A round twenty kilometers from Angers, surrounded by a large, deep moat making it appear to rest on a small island, the château of Plessis-Bourré, completely white under the shining slate roof, stands out in all its Renaissance splendour, which has remained intact throughout the centuries. Jean Bourré was in the service of the Dauphin Louis, son of Charles VII of France and when he became king in 1461, with the name of Louis XI, Bourré followed his fortunes, and was appointed Secretary of Finances and the Treasurer of France. A man of many interests, captivated by alchemy, Jean Bourré's creative spirit found its realization in the building of many spectacular châteaux (Langeais, Jazzé, Vaulx). In 1462, he purchased the Plessis-le-Vent estates from Charles de Ste-Maure and, six years later, began work on his new château, the only one he built which has completely preserved its original features and which is, without doubt, one of the most beautiful and imposing of all the châteaux along the Loire. Completed in four years, the external structure looks like a fortress, with its rectangular perimeter emphasized at the corners by four towers (the tallest of which, the donjon, is 44 metres high), designed to remain outside the shooting range of any enemy guns, but also impregnable to direct assault, with moving stairways and towers, thanks to its high walls which are over 2 metres thick. A 43 metre bridge makes it possible to cross the moat, leading to a double drawbridge and the original 3 metre wide platform – an element almost exclusive to this château – which runs around the château

The statues of Charles VIII (XV c.).

and was used for positioning artillery. It is enough, however, to pass through the huge entrance gate and enter the vast internal courtyard (a surface area of 1360 sq.m.) to discover, behind the rough, fortified appearance, a splendid elegant Renaissance residence, still entirely furnished and decorated according to the wishes of Jean Bourré's wife, Marguerite de Feschal, five centuries ago. Corridors with low arched vaults, stairways and galleries follow on from each other leading to a charming procession of halls and rooms which had the honour of welcoming first Louis XI, in 1473, and then Charles VIII, in 1487.

There is the huge Louis XVI hall, in which the XVIII century furniture blends well with the d'Aubusson tapestries and the floral motifs realized as ornaments for the doors by the great cabinet-maker David d'Angers; the Louis XV hall, with the walls covered in elegant panels with floral motifs; the great hall, incredibly luminous and refined by splendid boiseries; the Parliament hall, which served as an imposing dining-room, with its monumental richly decorated fireplace, Flanders tapestries and wood-engraved Gothic door. On the first floor is the Guardroom, noted for its stupendous ceiling, unique of its kind, which offers one of the most beautiful examples of XV century art. In painted wood, it is divided into six large sections which are, in turn, divided into four hexagons developed around a central rhombus. A total, therefore, of twenty-four large pictures painted on a blue-green background depicting famous proverbs, allegorical figures, protagonists of French legends, humorous scenes, all marked with the most classical of alchemic symbology, to which all the statues adorning the room also clearly refer. Worthy of note again is the master bedroom, with its splendid and austere Renaissance furnishings; the library where over three thousand books are kept along a 36 metre gallery; and the chapel of Ste-Anne, containing interesting examples of sacred art. The large residential complex is equipped to this day with the old, well preserved service rooms, cellars in particular, and the attics located on the top floor, covered by the magnificent chestnut-wood trussed roofing, giving access to the patrol communication passages.

The fortunes of Plessis-Bourré appeared to decline after Jean Bourré decided to move to the château at Jazzé. But it was this "abandonment", together with its position far away from important roads, which led to the château being preserved in its integrity to the present day. It passed from owner to owner, from the Counts of Bièvres to the De Ruillé family – under whose control it came through the Revolution unharmed, unlike Jean Guillaume de la Planche de Ruillé, then lord of Plessis-Bourré who was executed –, to the notary Avenant (XIX century) – who was responsible for the restorations and decorations in the large halls and chapel –, to Henri Vaïsse, who purchased the château in 1911 and whose descendants still live there today. Plessis-Bourré was declared a national historical monument in 1931.

The Athanor, alchemic emblem of the philosophical cauldron.

153

ANGERS

S ituated on the shores of the Maine river, Angers was once inhabited by fierce Celtic peoples who tenaciously opposed Roman
penetration.
After the period of the Norman invasions (IX century) Fulk Nerra,
Count of Anjou, had a castle built here. This first stronghold was
replaced by a better furnished architectural complex built by Louis
IX, known as St-Louis, between 1228 and 1238, which was then
further enlarged by Louis I of Anjou and under Louis II of Anjou,
who had the Gothic chapel built.
The court of René of Anjou, known as the Good, regent of Sicily
and Jerusalem, resided here. A man of letters and benefactor of the
local community, he was fond of fêtes and tournaments which were
often held at the castle. In an illuminated manuscript which he
himself executed, René illustrated in words and images the pomp
that accompanied the tournaments in the castle of Angers.
The religious wars later led to the decline of the castle and Henry
III ordered it to be demolished in 1585. The cylindrical towers of
the pentagonal stronghold began to be torn down and the conical

The imposing cylindrical towers of the château of Angers.

Details of the tapestries inspired by St. John's Apocalypse.

roof and the upper part were dismantled. When Henry IV came to the throne the destruction came to a halt and Angers was the scene of the engagement of César de Vendôme with Françoise of Lorraine. The series of Apocalypse Tapestries, commissioned by Louis I, Duke of Anjou, in 1373, is now on exhibit inside the castle. This magnificent textile, originally 140 metres long, is based on cartoons by the painter Jean de Bandol, also called Hennequin de Bruges, and was woven by Nicolas Bataille. The series of panels which illustrate the "Book of Revelations" of St. John was in the archbishopric of Arles in 1400 and after 1474 in the church of St-Maurice in Angers. In 1782 the tapestries disappeared, to be recovered in 1848 by a canon, Joubert, who had them restored. Each panel is accompanied by the figure of St. John, who participates in and illustrates the scene. The original captions were removed during the XIX century restoration because of their poor state of preservation.

LOIRE CUISINE

*T*he cuisine of the Loire basin, with its dramatic estuary and the green valleys of the tributaries, is perhaps less well known than that of Lyon or Burgundy, or of Normandy or Alsace, but it is just as varied, delicious, genuine, and winning. A true festival for the palate, rich in temptations and surprises. It is no coincidence that this is the birthplace of the proverbial Tarte Tatin, so "surprising" as to have astounded even its creator!

The common denominator in cooking in the "Pays de Loire" is, naturally, the excellent freshwater fish (a category that here includes many species also associated with salt water, cooked in a thousand different ways: alose (shad), brochet (pike), carpe (carp), civelle (the delicious baby eels, called cèe in Tuscany), lamproie (lamprey eel), sandre (pike perch), and saumon (salmon). The gardens abound in vegetables, each according to its season; the pasturelands graze herds of goats, whose milk goes to make cheeses of great renown; the farms raise choice beef cattle and pigs, besides quality poultry, like the famous géline noire of Loches; and the woods are full of game.

Anjou and Environs (Choletais, Saumurois, and Maine)

Early produce includes a famous salad green, the *cornette d'Anjou*, but the prize for originality is won by the quaint *pommes tapées*, oven-dried apples flattened with a hammer to make them easier to store, in the era of the great sailing ships, in the galley. The region is famous for its great wines, white (Savennières), red, and sparkling alike, and also for its liqueur-like wines (Coteaux-du-Layon, Quarts-de-Chaume, Bonnezeaux). Angers is the home of Cointreau and of Guignolet, a cherry-based sweet liqueur. The wine of the region "collaborates" in creating typical fish dishes, like *lamproie etuvée* (cooked with sweet white wine) and the tasty *bouilleture d'anguilles* (which calls for red), and such desserts as *poires à l'angevine*. Among the desserts are the *crémets d'Anjou*, while one of the best among the fancy cakes and pastries is the celebrated *sablé* of Sablé-sur-Sarthe.

Markets are held at Angers (Place Leclerc), Brissac-Quincé, Les Rosiers, Montreuil-Bellay, Montsoreau, and Saumur.

Touraine

Among the typical products of the area is its abundant produce, including a particular type of basil; from the pastures comes the fammed *Sainte-Maure*, a cylindrical soft cheese rubbed with ash and run through with a stalk of straw so as to better hold its form when fresh. The delicate meat of the *géline noire*, a black-feathered hen recently reintroduced to the area, vie as to flavor with the *andouillette au Vouvray*, a veal-and-pork sausage cooked with local wine. The wines, among which the noble Vouvray, bear the names of historical castles: Touraine-Azay-le-Rideau, Touraine-Amboise, Chinon, Bourgueil, and Saint-Nicholas-de-Bourgueil. The cuisine here is certainly not the most suitable for weight-watchers; quite the contrary, we might say it challenges the diner with such dishes as *rillons* (pork tidbits caramelized in lard), *rillettes* (a sort of "pork jam" preserved in fat, also a key ingredient in an excellent savory pie), *géline à la*

Lochoise, and *sandre à la Vouvrillonne*. For dessert, a *nougat de Tours* with almonds and candied fruit.

Markets: Tours (Place des Halles and Boulevard Heurteloup), Amboise, Azay-le-Rideau (where a magical nocturnal market offers gastronomical specialties on the third Friday of the month between June and September, and where in the autumn is held the Foire aux Pommes), Chinon (the home – not by chance – of François Rabelais who, as we well know, was a true expert on gluttony and greed), Langeais, and Loches.

Orléanais, Sologne, and Environs (Beauce, Gâtinais, Vendômois)

If Orléans is famous for its vinegar and onions and Sologne for its asparagus and game, Gâtinais is equally so for its saffron. Besides the excellent lake fish, it also boasts superb cheeses, like the *pithiviers au foin*. Among the fine wines are the

new and the vintage reds, suitable for accompanying game, are Cheverny and Cour-Cheverny, and then there are those wily whites, which once you start drinking them... Regional specialties include *carpe à la Chambord, civet de marcassin,* and *faisan au chou;* for dessert, *cotignac* (or quince jam), *pithiviers* with almonds, and the renowned Tarte Tatin, about the origins of which the following story is told. One day, at the hotel of the sisters Tatin, at Lamotte-Beuveron not far from the Chateau de Chambord, the absent-minded cook Fanny managed to slide her apple pie into the oven upside-down, with the pastry crust on top and the apples underneath, so producing, by mistake, the exquisite caramelized *tarte* that has made culinary history.

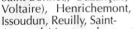

Berry and Environs (Brenne, Sancerrois)

The gardens and orchards of the area offer the typical green lentils, apples, and excellent honey; the pastures, goat-milk cheeses like the soft *crottin de Chavignol,* the *Pouligny-Saint-Pierre* with its blue-tinged crust, the *Selles-sur-Cher,* rubbed with ashes, and the *valençay;* the woods give us the walnut oil that was once used in place of butter as the most basic condiment. Justly famous are the white Sauvignon wines of Sancerre, as are the nectars of the outlying areas of Menetou-Salon, Quincy, and Reuilly. At table, there is a wide choice of dishes for both the vegetarians – *citrouillat,* savory squash pie, *galette de pommes de terre* – and "carnivores" among us: *pâté Berrichon* (a traditional Easter pie of mixed meats), *pintade au Reuilly* (guinea hen in white wine with grapes), *poulet en barbouille* (chicken cooked, at least if we follow the centuries-old recipe, in its own blood), and *gigot de sept heures* (leg of lamb, called thus in honor of the prolonged cooking time). For dessert, a sweet *Poirat.*

Markets: Argenton-sur-Creuse, Aubigny-sur-Nère, Bourges (Halles Saint-Bonnet), Buzançais, Châteauroux (Place de la Halle, Place Voltaire), Henrichemont, Issoudun, Reuilly, Saint-Armand-Montrond, and Valençay.

ALPHABETICAL INDEX